T0354505

The
Business
TextBook

..of the successful Branding and the creation
of a esteemed Flagship
quality business or store and of..

What came first
the Chicken or the Egg?

DEBORAH SHAUL

BALBOA.
PRESS
A DIVISION OF HAY HOUSE

Balboa Press books may be ordered through booksellers or by contacting:

Balboa Press
A Division of Hay House
1663 Liberty Drive
Bloomington, IN 47403
www.balboapress.com
1 (877) 407-4847

Print information available on the last page.

ISBN: 978-1-5043-3500-3 (sc)
ISBN: 978-1-5043-3502-7 (hc)
ISBN: 978-1-5043-3501-0 (e)

Library of Congress Control Number: 2015909975

Balboa Press rev. date: 10/30/2017

A comprehensive
Business Branding and
Flagship Store
Know How Book

What indeed came first, the Chicken or the Egg?

A book on teaching and transforming your thinking, into rethinking in the Godlike ways of implanting the egg inside the chicken, to assure continuance..and thereby, success in your businesses.

In business be ready for anything and everything to encompass your universallies and thereby get ready for life and success and everything better than yesterday and the day before and therefore I am here to start a revolution to masterly unobtrusively give light out to the world of business through helping and through advise that will hopefully change your very better prominent life time, just by reading this book.

What is the distinction and the antithesis and the contrast and of course, in a simpler formats the difference between Branding's and a Flagship store, or business?

A Branding is just recognition and identification and remembrance, just like the conceptual particles of the usages of sight words for pre-school children.

A flagship store, or business, is akin and in analogous and likened to a rubber stamp. Just, with the abilities to duplicate the impression and the imprint and the indentation of the stamp, as many times as you wish.

Index

Chapter One
The centurion questions of what came
    first the chicken or the egg?   1
Review   23

Chapter Two
The traumatizing news about our markups and our
    realer margins or truer profits written by a greater
    personality and a better partner in business.   35
Review   49

Chapter Three
The fallacies of cash flow   59
Review   81

Chapter Four
The distinctions between Branding and a
    Flagship Store or business...   93
Review   117

Chapter Five
Creating the infrastructure of the Flagship
    quality Stores or Businesses.   145
Review   171

Chapter Six
The art of "Piggybacking"   183
Review   205

Chapter Seven
Knowing your patrons   215
Midterm   227

Chapter Eight
What is the formulation for being a prominent
    businessman and woman in the formats of being
    a conductor and not in the orchestra?   241

Review   255

Final   265

Please realize that, everything that I have written is my ideologies and at times inspired by ideologies of my inspired loved ones and my communities predicaments in the astuter realms, of being a better business community and in the conducively better venues and habits, only of the recorded particles of the time lines of being in a better parts of my "channeled" from anyone, that cares about our planet and our country and therefore, our world at large.

I hereby, will just respond by saying that I am not a channeler, just astuter and care about everyone that is kind and well balanced and has love in their hearts for their very children and futures.

Chapter One

The centurion questions of what came
first the chicken or the egg?

You see, this auxiliary self help book, on business. In the similar and in a concordant proportionately grandeur way, of beginning with what I truly individualized and indoctrinated and of course my theoretical boomerang..

... of my philosophically outlandish views.

You see, I was blessed and truly ostracized my whole life for being a "know it all", when in reality I truly do, know it all...

Please realize that, because I was gifted and blessed with my puzzling ways and easily problem solving ways, on iluy staggering grade multifaceted venues of capabilities, on masterfully grandeur levels, of being able to understand and decipher and dissect and decode and unravel, where our business financial blockages and impediments are and where we are needed to alleviate and adjust and assemble, usually with just a few minor changes.

In this analogy, that is so apropos and so, in such a easier and alleviated ways of comprehensions..

Imagine, what a difference it would make to out couture pallets and our gourmet cuisines, by putting salt into your very greater meal. What a difference to our taste buds, that can be.

So, in my view points, these parts should be instituted in this book and in every further additional books, that I will be writing...

This formats will be advantageous in so many awe inspiring modus operandi ways and therefore, it should be my standardized venues, of every self improvement book's beginnings.

Ok.
What am I talking about?
The ideology of the prehistorically acclaimed formats of, *What came first the chicken, or the egg?*

You see, by developing the egg already in our business forum, or truly the conceptual parts of the developments, of the ideology and the paramountably greater, hopefully micro-niche market...

In the analogy and the philosophically greater and deeper understanding and personifications, of what came first the chicken, or the egg?...
By developing the egg, already in our business, in our beginning founding structures.. Programmations....

Let me give you a little background on whom I am.

You see, being that I am also a inspiring idealist and an imposingly better philosopher, I was contemplating being a grandeur particles of getting this book realized, in the acclimated parts of the scholastic greater world.

Please realize that I am also writing a book called "The Learning Disabled child of what came first the chicken or the egg?"..

I felt and deemed it necessary, that every book that I will be writing, I should commence and initiate my tutelage and my authentic teachings with the start with this formulation and concepts and intriguing parts, of being able to just procure the foundations of what we are involved in, at the very beginning of our creation process, or in the very start of the conception of our ideas, or in this very case, our business preludes.

So, get ready for this very understanding, of my interactively and in the Nationally Acclaimed question, of our centurion unknowns of our question, of "What came first the chicken, or the egg?"

The most popular particles of anything, that could ever be attributed to answering this questionnaire parts, is of the worst type of a let down, being that I am in the formats of knowing this answer, in the impressive ways possible.

So, here is a let down...

Because, I know the answer to the historically acclaimed asked question, of the time after time, over and over again, timeless question of what came first, the chicken, or the egg?...

By, the way this question is of the most importance to us, being as you will be seeing, in this very intriguing and very important parts of our studies, about the venue of us, as businessmen, or women, or wholesalers, or any part of doing your livelihood and thereby, your hopefully meaning, or purpose in life and therefore, our blessings in disguise and our presents in the forms of our Social talents...

Please realize that, to truly understanding the why's of our congegatings, of our unknown parts of our astuteness and our provocative venues, of our receiving's of these very greater answers, we are needed to truly individualize and understand that the answer to this centurion question, not only pertains to us, but is the "Founding Fathers" of every businesses.

It is the foundations and therefore, the nearer futuristically greater, God willing, prototype business and thereby, the "Flagship quality" Store or business, that I will be designing and instigating, in its very simpler formats of constructing and creating.

You see, the answer is of the simpler formats..

....that we never understood in the truer ways, but only in the greater ways of our never knowing, the truer answer.

We, have been guessing and hypothesizing and conjecturing at resolving this answer, from about eighty years and not counting anymore..

...and thereby, get ready for my version of the truer and unvarnished answer on how in pertains to our learning's and upgraded and newer ways of creating businesses, as it pertains to this appreciable answer..

In, reality, the answer to this timeless question is like a "duh?" to us..
.... Meaning, that it is in the very, very simplistic formats of our ways of thinking.

You see, if I were to be the inspired Creator and I was to be the ingenious businessman or woman, or virtuoso inventor, or imaginative patent creator, then I would be thinking about the end result and the offshoot, of how to grow and develop my very greater idea into quick monies, as well as for the nearer and futuristically farther Branding's and the creations of many brother or twin businesses, to accompany my Flagship quality businesses.

You see, again...
..if, I were to truly put myself into our God's mind and thereby...
Where, do you think I would be, at this point in time?

I, would be the one, that is thinking about my very beautiful world and my "Parnassa", in the Hebrew language my way of earnings and how I could appropriate this with my challenges and my very greater meaning and purpose in my lifetime, to serve and add value to our world.

I, would then start the "Creation Process", with the thoughts of the futuristically grandeur's of many parts of the venues...
... of the Evolution process.

In, the ways of..

....of, always having improvements and of up-grading systems, for my business.
For my monetary accumulations, to bare fruits for my enjoyments.

So, back to my analogy of the centurion question..

So, on behalf of all of you person's, that have never understood the philosophy of the Branding parts, of anything and everything...

...yes, every business needs to be branded and to be secured and visually realized and thereby, a very successful business.

You see, the trick, or the sport and greater skill, is never to minimize, or attenuate, or ever forget the importance and paramountcy, of adding technique to the mix, to assure, that even and especially the name..

The paramount importance..

Please realize that, the importance of attaining riches and paramountcy of attaining money exchanges and the vital parts of aggregating treasures and the truer crux, of succeeding at amassing capital and substantially greater monetary worth and the significance of bankrolling financial gains, is all in the preliminary intricacies of building your foundations of your business, or vocational outlet...

The name!!

The success without the expenditures of mass amount of monies for advertisements of your product or services, is the name, or the label, or in the products signature and trade name!!

You see, the importance and the priority of choosing a name, is to truly be able to identify and recognize and diagnosticate and thereby, understand and know right away, without a doubt, or dubiety, what the item, or the product, or the merchandise that you are selling is, or the service, is in it's entirety.

Just, by the name sake, that you have chosen to call your company, business, or store, or service...

Yes, it is funnier to make up catchy names, but how many of us get it?

It is not about your understanding, or your joke in the name sake. It is about branding and less advertising and coming up first on google, or on Amazon.

I once almost opened up a store called Chameleon and to me it was perfect. I wanted to keep on interchanging the merchandise and my very greater inventory..

It was a terrible and unfortunate idea. How would anyone, just by my name recognition, which is exactly what "Branding" is about, truly know, what kind of merchandise that I was selling? How long and how much more advertising, would I have needed to unveil, what I was wanting to sell and my stores "Branding" parts and therefore, have an influx of loyal customers?

You must realize, that this is one of our bigger mistakes in business. We derive and procure names, from pun on words, or rhymes or our family names and it seems like it is smart and fun and and witty, but it only makes the "Branding" parts of your business, more extensive and more aggrandized expenses and a farther harder sell and thereby, less business and reduced profits and unsubstantial bottom line and for sure a longer time period, until you are at that break even point.

You see, the emblem at the bottom of each page of this book format, is the greater emblem, that I hope to emblaze and to be remembered and to "Brand" and therefore, strategically place every where that I can without a doubt.

Just for learning purposes, I made the same mistake about fifteen years ago and counting, because "if I have to explain and emblem, then I did not make the right emblem to begin with".

So, just because maybe some of you are curious about my logo, or my emblem..

The girl is me, on a reserved platform of sharing, to free-her and more vivacious and more in the fashionistá venues of wearing blond curly hair, with her styling and flare..

The letter DCA are equalized in the proportionate particles of meaning, Divine Crown Attire.. this was my wig companies emblem and a mistake, but since energetically ten years past since the mistake was made, this emblem is already Branded..

Too much to explain and decipher? You then know and apperceived with certainty, that you made a fax paś with your emblem..

Does it pay for me to create and compose another emblem? No, unfortunately..

Like I just reiterated, the formats of the energetically perceivably ten year statutory time period of an overnight success processed..

Did I indeed err with this emblem?
Yes..
Did I have any overnight successes? Unfortunately, not perceivably by far.. so get ready to masterly hear of me, in a better formats of the creation processes.

You see, Emblems need to be self explanatory and in a moments glance, understood what wares are being sold, or dispensed of..

Another parts of for sure successes and another addition of the tricks, or concealments and stratagems, is to assure that whatever venue you are venturing into, if the product, or the service is needed by the world, or adds value to our formats of living, then you will have a "for sure" success and an assured and a steadfast favorable outcome. In this case the world will send you everything that you be needing to be a success.

..if we conceivably, in any formats of any giving back and recompense, to ourselves and our society, as a homogeneous congregation and we create and generate meaning and purposes, on an astuter parts of being in any preeminent venues, of us adding a leading value and regard and gain and beneficiallies to our very family, as well as our very egregious communities and our primary State and our notable Country and our flourishing world and of course our masterly surpassing universallies.

You see, the rewards, or the reverberations of caring about yourself and your family and your community and your state and your country and your world is...
..get ready for attainments and advancements and of course "buckets full" of financial gain, as a more attractive repercussion and a natural consequences, of adding value and expanding and supplementing superlative energetically greater formations, into our world.

In such a case, "the world your oyster".

So, this parts is where I tell you my philosophical translations, to the centurion question of "what came first the chicken or the egg?"

A little background first...
You see, in the process of reinventing and restructuring and creating a structural program, for our very businesses..

...I, have started writing this book, with the egg inside the thought processes, of our businesses betterments and their very "Founding Father" Flagship quality foundations and their very "aberdeen successes" and their greater superlative expansions and their extensively titanic technologically gettings, into the era of the time warp, of "The Jetsons", or "Star Trek" from the go..

...from, just the conception, of the idea of this book. From just the title of these publications...

To stimulate success. To purchase less advertisements. To grow a faster successful business or service...
..and to better understand, just from the title, or signature, what we are trying to sell quickly and efficiently.

THAT IS WHAT BRANDING IS ALL ABOUT!!

"NAME RECOGNITION"

By, me "Branding" this book and creating, a "Flagship-Type" of structure, by further putting the same formats of what came first the chicken or the egg, in every self help book that I write? And thereby, and in these exceedingly different ways of thinkings..

You see, what I have done with this book, is to release my logo at the bottom of this book, so that everyone will recognize this symbol and emblem and insignia, by the time that they have finished reading this format, of this book..

You see, again, by making you all anticipate and assemble and prepare and re-train, ourselves to think in advance..

By branding ourselves at the beginning, just like the egg is already implanted in the chicken anticipating greatness and birthing itself to a full grown chicken, that can procreate and have even preeminent future generations.

In return, instigating advancements and cash flows and reciprocates and standardizations, of only using "micro-niche" markets in every business.

Create with thoughts and intelligences, for the future of our businesses..

Teachings and guiding our future businessmen and our next generation businesswomen, into the ways of thinking, that only greater CFO's and masterfully greater personifications, would have ever dreamed of thinking about, in their very fifties..

..FLAGSHIPS, AND FLAGSHIP-TYPE STRUCTURES WITH ADDITIONAL STORES, AND MORE OUTLETS FOR EVERY OCCUPATION=more dollars.

.... and in a much grandeur personifications and esteemed target practices..

Yes, I know that it sounds, "a little out there."

But, by "Branding" our businesses, or occupations, or even ourselves, as I have talked about in my other book called, "Learning Disabled children and what came first the chicken or the egg?"

You see, we are needed at the very beginning of the creation process, of very creations of our businesses...

Even, teaching them the ways of Branding themselves, through the thought processes of manifestations.

In Manufacturing this very Program, I thought about the future of our business world, at a very tender parts of the conceptual particles of the thought process..

Before the opening of your business. During the creations of the energy of the namesake of your business.

You see, just, like God did...
When, He created the chicken, with the egg inside the chicken, ready to hatch and start, another generation of chickens, so that "the future is our's to see," with ease and of course, us not messing up His very creations and cooking the egg, before it hatches and not, realizing that Southern Fried Chicken was on the menu, too.

Yes.
I pray that I will be the one to guide and to transform our businesses with their already implanted seeds, in it's structure of any type, or formats of earning a living, or simply implanted in any venue whatsoever, of earnings.

Just like our God created the chicken, with the egg already inside the chicken.

It is God's nature, to always have the future in it's original fruit, to always think and create the futuristically masterfully greater sectionates, at the beginning and at the forefront of any parts of our creations, because God likes to masterly give and award and assure, that we and our continuance and the better particles of the future subsequent generations, are secure in the future.

Like the apple, or the avocado, or the grapes, or the olives and each fruit, has it's seed already implanted and embedded in it's very greater fruit...

... and thereby, we must do the same with our very extraordinary presents, of our talents and thereby, our earnings, or any parts of their masterly formulated offsets and for sure the namesake and every parts of the packaging and merchandising.

..and thereby, we facilitate developing and evolving the very grandeur ideas and designs and masterly subjugate and articulate and develop intrinsically in the time slots, that are their very better performa, without spending a Trillion Dollars like Coca Cola, or Oscar Meyer Weiner on advertisements.

You see, the natural progression, of the ways of our world is that we all want to advance, enrich, and develop and evolutionize..

..better lives and more acclamations, of the physical pleasures and luxuries, in every parts of our lives.

..by reformatting, into another up-graded and up-dated and elevated versions, of what is beyond the norm, of what is truly in the lluy parts of your industry.

Please, truly individualize and understand, that if there is going to be long-term and abiding and incessantly superlative successes, then every year, you MUST up-grade and ameliorate and promote and reclaim and invest time and monies, in your very business.

You see, approximately 13% of your NET profits, must go into up-grading and redressing and the renovations of your store, or your show rooms and definitely your work spaces, every year, in order not to have a stagnant business and thereby, an energetically immobile, or dying business, God forbid.

There is also, the possibility and misfortune, in every business and this happened and occurred to me personally, with my very successful business...

Perhaps, you are in are in a dismal and lugubrious situation, of having your competitors up-grade and plagiarize, to your greater versions of your product and thereby, you must please, keep on forging ahead and evolving and be the innovator and the trendsetter and the trailblazer and of course, the austere leader of your industry and keep your competitors at arms length and at a disadvantage.

You see, there is another component in our businesses, that must be mentioned, understanding logic and understanding formats and structures and individualizing personifications of greater foundations and structures..

So, please understand that, I will be expanding on these very subject matters, in this book. I will be teaching and instructing you, in the simplest formats, for the assurance of our well thought out, easy starters and masterly faster performance gratas, in the bottom numbers of our manifestations of our NET profits.

....and thereby, in the more natural parts of the creation processes, or developing your educational structures, with the metaphorical egg, already inside of your chicken, so to speak.

We just need to nurture the "egg" that has already been planted and is in the incubation of the developing store, or business, or occupation, or service.

You see, I hope to achieve the parts, where I will explain to you, how to implant the egg, or the future parts of your very greater ideas and gifts of your talent, or the venue of producing anything for the futuristically greater monetary reasons, or for any development reasons, already securely implanted in the infrastructure and your very foundations of your occupation, or structural programs, of earning a greater living...

You see, in this ways your businesses, will not only be a grandeur and resplendence future prototype....

....but, we will have the security of knowing, that we have the structure of the egg inside our businesses, the natural growth of the future parts of our developmentally cocooned and nurtured businesses, as well as for the longevity and the ability to create "Branded" inventory, with a futuristically greater "Flagship type" professional particles, already implanted, for easier duplications and a much greater prefabrications of monetarily enhancing our very lives.

You see, because therefore, our lives will be less pressurizations and in a better "pre-approved" formulations, we will have more passions for our very better parts of their professional livelihoods. We will be adding an abundantly considerably greater value to ourselves, as well as eminence to our wives or husbands, and for sure calibrations to our better parts of our families.

Please, remember the greater esteem, that we will be appending to our communities, as well as for our the greater enhancements, of stimulating meaning to our States and exacting excellence, to our countries and never forget as a universallies, we add a better regard and valuation to our world.

If we secure your very greater foundations and the infrastructures of your business and assure, that your structures and your variants and the "Moving Parts" of your stores, are so well rooted and entrenched, that any negativities and any bumps, or hurdles in the road, will have little, or no effect, on your professional, as well as for their futuristically solid very self confidences and for sure, their very restructured parts of being a better personification..

... in the hopes of being at work for the same amount of hours, or maybe even lesser..
..just working smarter and getting much more results in a quicker time lapse, as well as, for so much less stress, because of the business module.

Please realize that, when our stores foundations are strong and secure and we instigate and acknowledge and foresee, exactly what is truly happening in every parts, of our departmental parts and in every segmented particles of our structured or non-structured ways of earning a living.

You see, we thereby, never are in any panic modes, of being in a turbulent and reconstructed time line of any distress from our stores, or businesses, from deteriorating and getting into any"neglect zones".

The better, that we become at understanding our businesses, the better that this world will be and thereby, please never forget to appreciate and to achieve and to institute so many greater products and inventory, into any society and any proportionately better unobstructed, better for us and our very greater world.

You see, we then will have the abilities and the virtues and the flexibilities, of being in the energetically greater flows of creations and thereby, patents and restructuring of our world, in such innovative and commercially sound, better for each individual and a higher standardization ways of living, will prevail.

Instead of the most glamorous Hotel being five stars, we can elevate our luxurious lives and our mundane to most, to eleven, or thirteen stars. We should be at this point in time be living in a "Jetsons" time periods, with a more obscure with more privacies and more industrializations and cathedral and palatial-like automized and robotically run, homes.

Imagine, you earning a greater NET profits and thereby..

That is one of my goals!
Yes it sounds ridiculous...
But, so did flying an airplane.

So, here is my Plan, to aspire to this probability.

It is all in the Branding's of each allocated professional parts, from a younger stages and tender parts of your conceptual "idea". It is all about in preparations, of developing a sound aspiring "micro-niche" and a love of doing what you are inspired to do or to be, at this point in your very greater lives.

Chapter One

Review

1. What is all the hype about the philosophically centurion question, of what came first the chicken or the egg, and why is it of such a caliber of importance, in the commencements of a staggeringly Flagship Quality store, or business structure, or paragon?

_____

_____

_____

_____

_____

_____

_____

_____

_____

_____

_____

_____

_____

_____

_____

_____

_____

_____

_____

_____

_____

_____

_____

2. What does it truly imply and further refer to, to Brand your businesses name?

_____

_____

_____

_____

_____

_____

_____

_____

_____

_____

_____

_____

3. What is this the new age standardizations, of nstigating profits, in a shorter epigrammatic amounts of time periods?

_____

_____

_____

_____

_____

_____

_____

_____

_____

_____

_____

_____

_____

4. What are the Flagship Quality Store fundamentalities and axiological and of course the oxiomatic core infrastructures?

_____

_____

_____

_____

_____

_____

_____

_____

_____

5. Please, acquaint me about what are the fundamental particles and requisites to structure and configure and erect, a Branding that does not eat away at your profits?

_____

_____

_____

_____

_____

_____

_____

_____

_____

_____

_____

_____

_____

_____

6. Please, communicate to me, how do we truly facilitate and collaborate and abate the impediments of imbedding the egg inside the chicken, in your business apparatus and conceivably interrelated structures?

_____

_____

_____

_____

_____

_____

_____

_____

_____

_____

7. Please, commission desiderate and cull a business and describe and chronicle and please also delineate and portray, how you can best achieve...
   1. A preeminent Branding, without diminution and gourmandizations and without eating at your profits and at your NET capitalizations.

_____

_____

_____

_____

_____

_____

_____

_____

_____

_____

_____

_____

_____

_____

2. A transcendent and supreme Flagship Quality Business framework and methodologies and of course ecosystems and complexities.

_____

_____

_____

_____

_____

_____

_____

_____

_____

_____

_____

_____

_____

_____

_____

_____

_____

_____

8. Please, choose a Store type and describe how you can best achieve...

   1. A Branding programmation and habitus and systematization, without abating and reducing and attenuating the NET of your emoluments and valuable profits.

   _____

   _____

   _____

   _____

   _____

   _____

   _____

   _____

   _____

   _____

   _____

   2. An inordinate Flagship Quality Store composition and gestalt foundations.

   _____

   _____

   _____

   _____

   _____

   _____

   _____

   _____

   _____

   _____

   _____

   _____

_____

_____

_____

_____

_____

_____

_____

_____

_____

9. Please, predestine a Service oriented business type and blazon and quintessence that permeates and describes how you can best achieve...
   1. A superlative Branding, without eating or attenuating at your NET profits?

_____

_____

_____

_____

_____

_____

_____

_____

_____

_____

_____

_____

_____

_____

_____

_____

2. A colossal Flagship Quality Service conformation structure.

_____

_____

_____

_____

_____

_____

_____

_____

_____

_____

_____

10. Please commit to an E-Commerce type of a well-regulated methodized structured business and describe and evaluate how you can best achieve...
    1. A Branding without curtailing the influx of your NET profits.

_____

_____

_____

_____

_____

_____

_____

_____

_____

_____

_____

_____

2. A extensive quality Flagship Quality E-Commerce complex structure.

Chapter Two

The traumatizing news about our markups and our realer margins or truer profits written by a greater personality and a better partner in business.

Oy!

Hi, my name is Johnson and I am the one in unison and in conjunction with this writer, that is alleviating and co-writing, this very harder than normal chapter.

You see, being that I have Port Authority expertise, I am required to transcribe for my friends and colleagues this chapter, in order to under establish the evaluations of our businesses, being that our numbers and our cost effective particles, are so under estimated..

Ugh!!
Please realize that, most of us are in peril of going bankrupt, because we are using and appropriating our cash flow, to barely stay afloat and after you read my chapter on the usages of cash flow, you will discern and truly be cognizant of and conceivably realize, that ultimately and therefore, somewhen and eventually, we have to "pay the piper" and our expenditures and our invoices and our debt pile up and the reckoning and the over flow catches up..

Please realize that, this writer is not interested in publishing this chapter, because, it is such a discouraging chapter and thereby, please realize, that unfortunately this scenario is true and real and vicariously, in the mass parts of being called in for larceny.

This is an unyielding and more difficult chapter than most, to allocate and to conjure and explain and teach and guide you all, to the best of our abilities.....

Please, note that most of you are either starting businesses, or already in a business structure.

You see, you must understand, that there is so much misunderstandings, when it comes to aggregated business structures.

For the start, to truly understand our payment structures...

There is no such monster, that does not pay for their goods anymore. We must pay COD, or "Prepay", through PayPal and UPS and other sources..

What happened to trust?

What happened to success?

What happened to *"Asteria Lane"* from a time slot of the [1]*"Stepford Generation"?*

What was the first thing, that was ever truly understood, concerning the easier playful lives and therefore, a *"ball of wax"* kind of feelings of happiness?

---

[1]   What does it take to become a Stepford wife, a woman perfect beyond belief? Ask the Stepford husbands, who've created this high-tech terrifying little town, in a very modern comedy-thriller.
Director: Frank Oz
Writers: Ira Levin (book), Paul Rudnick (screenplay)
Stars: Nicole Kidman, Bette Midler, Matthew Broderick | See full cast & crew"

Is there such a thing as happiness in life and in securities and in sleeping at night, when you own a business?

Did you know that, there is no such thing as a greater business success in a small store, unless the markup is over 90% percentile? If an item is $10 the sale price needs to be $19 just to break even!!

Please be ready to upgrade, all you small stores!! Best wishes to all of you hard workers, all of you mom and pop stores and to all of of you holding back on too much stock and inventory!! Please stop!! You have your money in a bad investment place, as we will be talking about in this chapter.

Beware, you have all of your profits in your inventory, according to everyone.

You see, that is how my friend felt and now, he is sleeping at night and now he is in the point of his life of retiring and selling his business.

My anonymous friend, is writing this parts...

Oy!
There was a juncture in my very busy time period, that in my store, I had a "friends and family", that literally abducted every piece of every greater preeminent name brand merchandise that was on my selling receptacles, or racks of merchandise, that they could possibly find in their sizes and any size for that matter..

This "friends and family plan", took all of my crème de la crème au courant inventory, that barely saw the light of day..

This "friends and family plan," had little consternation that the garments were too small, or too large, or just was not for their body type..

They compasses and "abducted" everything, thinking that my wholesale price was like a bargain basement structure of their receiving's, of such a better deal, which they never reimbursed me for, in any case.

You see, the mentalities of a sale consumer, is that even if the merchandise is not quite right, or that they were not needing this type of product, they purchase it anyway, in thinking that "oh my God look at the price!!"

So, my terrible luck, as they convoyed everything, that they could muster and yes, they barely requested and desiderated to pay me the wholesale price and all I could say was, "Please, just delight and regard and take pleasure and enjoy!".

You see, I did not conceivably fathom in any design, or depict in any habitude, or perceive in any modus operandi, or imagine in any contrivance, or in unspecified modicum, of any time lapses, that I would be over paying and that it is necessary to cover my inventories, with approximately anther 90 percentile, extra monies, on top of the wholesale price, that I had been paying and even astoundingly greater more revenues are necessary, after the payments of rent and other expenditures that need to be incorporated in the wholesale price.

Please realize that, that would not include my warehouse expenditures, of an added precipitation and astronomically abundantly 90 percentile additions, being that I require trucking and employees and inventory and rentals and a secretary and the maintenance staff and of course, not to forget "[2]working capital", just to break even and therefore, Oy and Oy again!!

You see, the contrivance and the stratagem is...
Ok.
In plain English.

The story is that, not withstanding and with a lack of support from all of my family and friends, I am on the verge of bankruptcy and I will enumerate and expand on this subject shortly.

So, every time that My "friends and family" helped themselves to and snared the best of what came in for the new season and attained every part of the crème de la crème mass parts of every style that they wanted, I was at a much extensive deficit and towering loss, than I ever could have known, or disclosed, or ever imagined.

You see, I figured that they all took about 20% percentile of my given "cream of the crop" or the choice parts of

---

[2] My personal definition is that, any monies that you have put aside, to enhance your business, to advertise, or to create an enhanced business or environment.

my inventory and therefore, just an example, I had a $1,000,000 in stock...

I thought that they just took about $200,000...

But, guess what? I lost on that "friends and family plan", about $560,000, but being that it cost me approximately 180% percentile, just to break even !!

You see, the wholesale premium, or price was approximately $200,000 and it's the additional expenditures, of approximately 180% percentile margin of my wholesale price, to just break even, which puts my wholesale cost truly at $560,000.

You see, that add up to in totalities $560,000, instead of the wholesale premium of $200,000, that my friends and family arrogated and "high jacked" from my retail divisions of my businesses.

Imagine that!!

Let me explain to you how this happened. If I have an inventory of $1,000,000, four times a year, I needed to understand, that it cost me about 90% for my expenditures and my outlay and my partial burden of my overhead, for my very trying at times business.

Please realize that, I also must require an extra allotments of approximately another configuration of 90% percentile, because of my storage facilities outlay and my trucking disbursements and my warehousing liabilities and every expenditure, that is associated with these parts of wholesaling....

Just, to break even.

Imagine that!!
Please understand that, I will expenditurize the extravagantly sadder expenditures, that it truly takes to earn a profit, for learning and research and knowledge purposes, as we will be attaining and understanding, in this chapter.

Let us start by explaining to you, how much it really takes to break even.

Every business needs inventory, so if you are purchasing your stock, or inventory, or merchandise from any "Export Region', please realize that, we mostly pre-pay approximately 1/4 of your said "order", or merchandise with PayPal, with our credit cards.

Here is the breakdown on $1,000,000 in inventory.

PayPal charge is 4% percentile=$40,000.

Just by the usages of your Credit card, the charge is approximately another 3% percentile, so add another =$30,000.

If you are pre-paying and do not pay back the balance on your credit card, the average percentile per annum is approximately anywhere from 13%-25% percentile. The

added cost in this case for the merchandise would be an extra
$130,000-$250,000.

Not to forget, shipping charges are in the astronomical range of 30% percentile, from any foreign countries.

Now, depending on your street savvy particles, of making sure that you are not overpaying for shipping and handling charges. Almost, everyone of us are paying 30% percentile at the total cost of $300,000.

This payment of shipping is most probably only to the port and therefore, we have to hire a shipping company, that will charge us another minimum $20,000, which equates to 2%.

New York State licenses taxes and other augments charges at the Port Authority are approximately 5% percentile for taxes and another $100,000 for each container for relinquishing the merchandise at a timely span of time. The total for this reciprocations are $50,000 for taxes and another 10% percentile, or $100,000 for the lubrication process. In totalities, that $150,000.

So, from the span of time of your order of $1,000,000, until your actualities of your finally freighting and enjoy and delivery to your warehouse, the cost and expenditures are in the rate, or the tariff, of approximately so far 79% percentile, or 790,000, for expenses for an inventory of $1,000,000, plus, we have to add on the window treatments and the merchandise, that is in the window displays and the workers and the stained, or torn clothing, do to try ons and so much more..

Now, that we have transported and shipped your inventory and your to your reservoir and of course, your totalities of your stock to your depo, or warehouse, or depository, we now will be taking into consideration the lease agreement contract and the payroll for your assiduous and diligent employees.

Please realize, that we still have the outlay and the disbursements and the tariff of the taxes and the overhead, and losses that all add up to approximately 90% percentile of your inventories, or stocks NET worth.

You see, the price that you have paid for your merchandise, in this frightening and horrifying example of 90% percentile of a $1,000,000, would be an extra $900,000 for all your requirements and charges, until it reaches your retail location, which adds up to $1,900,000 instead of $1,000,000.

Now, to get to your retail location, you have that same trucking company at $20,000 adding another 2% on the expenditure side and hopefully your merchandise in tack.

Now that your inventory, has successfully made it to your retail store, you will be paying your taxes and your lease agreements and your managerial payrolls and the sales team's disbursements and your accountant surcharges and your cleaning help's output and your window treatments investments and your soon to be despised "sales rack", as we will be talking about.

Please calculate and asses the aggregated amounts and outlay and please discern and capitulate, that they are most probably, approximately 90% percentile of the original and the initial $1,000,000 totallying and equaling to $900,000.

So, after UPS, or any ground shipping company and our inventory or merchandise is in a retail location, with approximately $1,000,000 in inventory, we are amenable and liable for the amount of about $1,900,000..

Our mark up, thereby, has to be 1.8 times the whole sale price, or 180% margin, just to break even.

If your wholesale price is $10 just to break even you must charge $28, just to break even and if this item goes on sale, we will lose money, if we do not keep in mind the truer evaluation, of what we are truly paying per including our overhead.

Now, please remember and be cognizant of the fact, that if you have a warehouse, or a storage facility, then you are liable for the same $1,000,000's in merchandise, another 90% percentile, tallying, or adding up to $2,800,000 for your inventory, if you are luckier than most, just to break even.

..so, a $1 item, really is costing you $2.80 wholesale, just to break even.

You see the problem arises when you have truly thought that you paid let's say $1 for an item and thereby, the value or the worth of the item to you retail might be about $2-$3 but now your whole sale price is $2.80 and therefore if you want to receive profits of "doubling" or adding a 100% margin as a markup the price of this same "$1" item becomes $5.60, which no one will purchase being that the evaluation of that product is much lower and a cheap looking item.

How is that possible..

You see, please realize that I am just a friend of Deborah's and I am here to enlighten and expound and catechize her in the realer ways of our imports, although, she also has experience and involvement and empiricisms, in made in China goods and has experienced and has been there for her own business, many times..

... and now, please refresh our memories... imagine then, the extra tariff from our terrible President..

Imagine, with all of our businesses and investments and enterprises, toppling down, capsizing, teetering out of control and uncontainable, without restraint, like a "House of cards"...

And then..
Unimaginable!!

A supplementary and further tax and levy, for all imports! Imagine, that!!

"I will huff and I will puff" said President Donald Trump "and I will blow your house down".

I must enlighten and instill knowledge and catechize to you all, that if you want to purchase, or acquisition goods in china, or even procure merchandise in Alaska, Or commit to any inventory from Hawaii..

Please, I bequeath upon you to acquire and contract and purchase it from New York and pay more. Please, realize that you are not understanding, that even the wholesalers and factories are regarding purchasing and bearing the cost, of so much more than they surmise and conceivably think and guesstimate that they are being charged and, for each piece of inventory..

Please realize, that even in a basement shop, or a restaurant operation, or a building mega corp, or a hotel, these numbers are realer, than we even can ever truly imagine.

Even, Israel and England and Italy and France and every country, charged the same charges, being that everything today is made is
China and that everything, is manufactured in Chinese factories.

Please, take into account this important and this crucial verbatim chapter and just, apply and endow to yourselves, an acceptable amount of net profits to exceed the break even points, which we only talked about in this ponderous to scribe and to evaluate and collate this chapter.

Be great and live and love and travel and be happier.
Love Johnson

Chapter Two

Review

1. Please, disclose and annotate, what "working capital", truly means?

_____

_____

_____

_____

_____

_____

_____

_____

_____

_____

_____

_____

_____

_____

_____

_____

_____

_____

_____

_____

_____

_____

_____

_____

_____

_____

_____

2. Please paraphrase and unravel the misconceptions of what "working capital" truly mean to a business personality?

_____
_____
_____
_____
_____
_____
_____
_____
_____
_____
_____
_____

3. Please, construe and clarify, one example of a company and itemize every expense and figure out and itemize and disclose, what markup your product, or service must require, in order to masterly just break even?

_____
_____
_____
_____
_____
_____
_____
_____
_____
_____
_____

4. Please, annotate and break down, what markup did you achieve and thereby explicate, from the last exercise, number three.

5. _____
   _____
   _____
   _____
   _____
   _____
   _____
   _____
   _____
   _____

6. Please, give reason for and justify, if you did not end up with an amount closer to 90% and therefore, please, seek and resolve the missing other miscellaneous expenses, that you did not take into account, for example taxes..

   _____
   _____
   _____
   _____
   _____
   _____
   _____
   _____
   _____
   _____
   _____
   _____
   _____

7. Please, disclose and account for, how does the "family plan" effect your business in a destructive formats, even if you mean well and you are generous. Even, your immediate family structure can disrepair your Company?

_____
_____
_____
_____
_____
_____
_____
_____
_____
_____
_____
_____
_____
_____
_____
_____
_____
_____
_____
_____
_____
_____
_____

8. Please, disclose and elucidate what is the realer Cost of purchasing inventory from abroad and refine and commentate, how do we received that number?

_____

_____

_____

_____

_____

_____

_____

_____

_____

_____

_____

_____

_____

_____

_____

_____

_____

_____

_____

_____

_____

_____

_____

_____

Chapter Three

The fallacies of cash flow

How do I exonerate and assimilate and appropriate, that when we boast and possess a business, it is so inherently and vitally important, to have a separation between "Church and State", between your business monies and your personal income.

Ugh!
I suffer from this ailment as well...

You see, regardless of whether we own a "Mom and Pop" business, or we have a considerably and mammoth husky business, that we are nurturing and expanding and burgeoning into a mega Corp, or a dynasty empire and that we are growing, every penny and the entireties of every particle of your inventory, must me accounted for and kept tabs on and appraised. Every cash register and every till and every dollar that is spent, even if it is for supplies, or a business lunch, or a taxi ride to your appointment, must be acknowledged and verified and written down.

In order to truly understand your expenditures and thereby, truly individualize what the markup, or margin MUST BE, in order to actuate an even modest profited income, we are needed to account for every single dollar amount and every single piece of inventory that has been credited, in any format whatsoever..

Even the losses from the "Family plan"..

Please, get ready never to touch your cash box, or your inventory, ever again and thereby, never destroy your business ever again.

Before anything else, I do not know how to explain it, except in the most simplistically greater formats..

By retrieving and repossessing monies, or revenues, out of your cash box, or by utilizing any of your bankroll, or your monies, or stock, or inventory, in essence you are "stealing" or depleting monies from yourselves and your own businesses.

How is that possible?

Let me explain...

These fragile and feeble and delicate businesses, especially for the first five years, can not handle any disruption of funds and capital, or inventory, or anything that has any monetary value, in any parts that would topple the bookkeeping spread sheets and bankroll, to the red..

..or for that matter not know exactly the whereabouts of every dollar spent and earned..

You see, you might think that you are doing well, because there is a tremendous amount of cash flow from the inventory sales and from the cash registers availabilities, which are usually only in the partiallies of the truer [3]operating cash flows.

---

[3]   Operating cash flow Wikipedia
       In financial accounting, operating cash flow (OCF), cash flow provided by operations, cash flow from operating activities (CFO) or free cash flow from operations (FCFO), refers to the amount of cash a company generates from the revenues it brings in, excluding costs associated

Oy!
This happened to me also.

First of all let me explain and achieve a greater understanding on what operating cash flow, or OCF, in the direct correlation of [4]EBITDA, or in my easier ways

---

with long-term investment on capital items or investment in securities. [1] The International Financial Reporting Standards defines operating cash flow as cash generated from operations less taxation and interest paid, investment income received and less dividends paid gives rise to operating cash flows.[2] To calculate cash generated from operations, one must calculate cash generated from customers and cash paid to suppliers. The difference between the two reflects cash generated from operations.
Operating Cash Flow vs. Net Income, EBIT, and EBITDA ~

Interest is an operating flow. Since it adjusts for liabilities, receivables, and depreciation, operating cash flow is a more accurate measure of how much cash a company has generated (or used) than traditional measures of profitability such as net income or EBIT. For example, a company with numerous fixed assets on its books (e.g. factories, machinery, etc.) would likely have decreased net income due to depreciation; however, as depreciation is a non-cash expense[3] the operating cash flow would provide a more accurate picture of the company's current cash holdings than the artificially low net income.[4]

Earnings before interest, taxes, depreciation and amortization (EBITDA) is a non-GAAP metric that can be used to evaluate a company's profitability based on net working capital. The difference between EBITDA and OCF would then reflect how the entity finances its net working capital in the short term. OCF is not a measure of free cash flow and the effect of investment activities would need to be considered to arrive at the free cash flow of the entity.

4   Earnings before interest, taxes, depreciation, and amortization Wikipedia

A company's earnings before interest, taxes, depreciation, and amortization (commonly abbreviated EBITDA,[1] pronounced /

to understand this term, it means Gross operating cash flows or OCF before all of the added expenditures that

---

iːbɪtˈdɑː/,[2] /əˈbɪtdɑː/,[3] or /ˈɛbɪtdɑː/[4]) is an accounting measure calculated using a company's net earnings, before interest expenses, taxes, depreciation and amortization are subtracted, as a proxy for a company's current operating profitability (i.e., how much profit it makes with its present assets and its operations on the products it produces and sells, as well as providing a proxy for cash flow).

Although EBITDA is not a financial measure recognized in generally accepted accounting principles, it is widely used in many areas of finance when assessing the performance of a company, such as securities analysis. It is intended to allow a comparison of profitability between different companies, by discounting the effects of interest payments from different forms of financing (by ignoring interest payments), political jurisdictions (by ignoring tax), collections of assets (by ignoring depreciation of assets), and different takeover histories (by ignoring amortization often stemming from goodwill). EBITDA is a financial measurement of cash flow from operations that is widely used in mergers and acquisitions of small businesses and businesses in the middle market. It is not unusual for adjustments to be made to EBITDA to normalize the measurement allowing buyers to compare the performance of one business to another.[5]

A negative EBITDA indicates that a business has fundamental problems with profitability and with cash flow. A positive EBITDA, on the other hand, does not necessarily mean that the business generates cash. This is because EBITDA ignores changes in working capital (usually needed when growing a business), in capital expenditures (needed to replace assets that have broken down), in taxes, and in interest.

Some analysts do not support omission of capital expenditures when evaluating the profitability of a company: capital expenditures are needed to maintain the asset base which in turn allows for profit. Warren Buffett famously asked: "Does management think the tooth fairy pays for capital expenditures?"[6]

EBITDA margin refers to EBITDA divided by total revenue (or "total output", "output" differing "revenue" by the changes in inventory).[7]

would make it a "NET Cash Flow", in my easier ways to understand this particular chapter...

You see, the truer and simplistic meaning of "Cash flow", is just a generation of cash, that is achieved through the sales of the "goods" or your inventory. This can be achieved either in the wholesale distribution parts of the spectrum, AKA wholesalers, or this can be procured by the normal to overwhelming sales of your inventory on a day to day basis, or on a negatively based formats of sales, as I wish that I had time to expand on. This subject needs a whole other formatted book. Let us see.

Anyway, these very cash flows are the accumulations of the cost plus the profits of your merchandise and thereby, are mostly, approximately 90%-180% of the monies that you are earning, or annex as cash flows, and the totalities of payments and indemnifications, that are under your obligations of disbursements beholden and that you owe and are in debts and under obligations, as a result of some cost and expenditures, or overhead, up until that very point in time, or simply EBITDA.

You see, these expenditures and "bills" can even elapsed by many previous centennial in the mortgage departments, or foregoing [5]liens on properties, or former [6]annuities, or

---

[5]   Lien Wikipedia
      For other uses, see Lien (disambiguation).
      A lien (/ˈliːn/ or /ˈliːən/)[Note 1] is a form of security interest granted over
      an item of property to secure the payment of a debt or performance
      of some other obligation. The owner of the property, who grants the
      lien, is referred to as the lienee[3] and the person who has the benefit
      of the lien is referred to as the lienor[4] or lien holder.

      The etymological root is Anglo-French lien, loyen "bond", "restraint",
      from Latin ligamen, from ligare "to bind".

      In the United States, the term lien generally refers to a wide range of
      encumbrances and would include other forms of mortgage or charge.
      In the USA, a lien characteristically refers to non-possessory security
      interests (see generally: Security interest—categories).

      In other common-law countries, the term lien refers to a very specific
      type of security interest, being a passive right to retain (but not sell)
      property until the debt or other obligation is discharged. In contrast
      to the usage of the term in the USA, in other countries it refers to a
      purely possessory form of security interest; indeed, when possession
      of the property is lost, the lien is released.[5] However, common-law
      countries also recognize a slightly anomalous form of security interest
      called an "equitable lien" which arises in certain rare instances.

      Despite their differences in terminology and application, there are a
      number of similarities between liens in the USA and elsewhere in the
      common-law world.

[6]   Annuity Wikipedia
      For other uses, see Annuity (disambiguation).
      An annuity is a series of equal payments at regular intervals. Examples
      of annuities are regular deposits to a savings account, monthly home
      mortgage payments, monthly insurance payments and pension
      payments. Annuities are classified by the frequency of payment dates.
      The payments (deposits) may be made weekly, monthly, quarterly,
      yearly, or at any other interval of time.

      An annuity which provides for payments for the remainder of a
      person's lifetime is a life annuity.

other prior importuned investments, or just simply, an "extinct" non-disclosure agreement, of making deals with the banks for extended dues of merchandise, or the far reaching reckoning of rents on your store, or leasing's on your business, or forgotten worker compensations and maybe, even some future, or bygone pensions plans.

So, here we go...
Let's say...
Imagine, you retrieved $10,000 from "cash flow" and now you owe monies and you have not finished paying the window displays, or the garbage disposals, or the last payments on the clothing, or your inventory..

Oy!!
You owed $20,000 instead of $10,000 that you spent and took those funds from your "cash flow" and now you are in a deficit of over $20,000 for now, until you go for "more cash flows" that truly belong to the business.

Please, if necessary give yourself a salary instead, even if your business is in the negative, so that you will truly understand and know, what monies belong to the business and what monies are profits.

You see, I am an aspiring Energyst...
How is that important to you to articulate and to truly individualize?

You must know that, this information and absolutely and authentically scary data, that I am about to explain to you all, is of utmost value to your lives, because you live in an energetic world, with energy, whether you like it or not.

The factual parts of how the energy of money and the energy of doing business effect us and our world, in such greater ways.

Get ready, for this fascinating information...
You see, there is such a thing as energy in our entirety of our world.

As a matter of fact, the whole ensemble of our Universallies also consists and contains energy. Everything out there has energy, to some degree!!

Imagine that!!

You see, let me explain how energy works and creates and is activated...

Let me explain and reiterate...

Money is energy. This is a concept and an abstraction and a philosophical view point, that was taught and revealed to me, over eight years ago.

Please realize that, it starts simply with the fact that everything and I mean everything is energy.

[7]Matter is just energy, some better positively based energy and unfortunately a portionate parts of negatively based energy.

You see, money is a neutral energetically compound...

Imagine, just like paper. It formulates the energetically mediocre formats of acting energetically "just" like the paper and the ink energy that it formulates, before the printing processes of our monies...

We can transform and recreate and reformulate and restructure the energy of money, with the usage of our currencies..

It just depends, on how we channel our finances and route our assets, or aqueduct our funds, in order to create goodness, or God forbid reek havoc and formulate corruption energy. It is always contingent and predominant and preponderant on what medium, or conduit, or duct, the monies are funneled through and transported by way

---

[7]   Matter Wikipedia
       Matter is usually classified into three classical states, with plasma
       sometimes added as a fourth state. From top to bottom: quartz (solid),
       water (liquid), nitrogen dioxide (gas), and a plasma globe (plasma).
       In the classical physics observed in everyday life, if something has
       mass and takes up space, it is said to be composed of matter; this
       includes atoms (and thus molecules) and anything made up of these,
       but not other energy phenomena or waves such as light or sound.
       [1][2] More generally, however, in (modern) physics, matter is not a
       fundamental concept because a universal definition of it is elusive:
       elementary constituents of atoms may not take up space individually,
       and massless particles may be composed to form objects that have
       mass (even when at rest).

of what intermediary of energy and conveyed into what segment of energy, that we are utilizing, our monies with.

You see, the normal consistencies, or makeup of our money is that everything is energy based, so once a minutely small amount of [8]negative energy, even a trace amount of unfavorable energy is removed from our monies, this

---

[8]   Wikipedia
       Negative energy is a concept used in physics to explain the nature of certain fields, including the gravitational field and a number of quantum field effects.

       In more speculative theories, negative energy is involved in wormholes which allow time travel and warp drives for faster-than-light space travel.

       Main article: Gravitational energy
       The strength of the gravitational attraction between two objects represents the amount of gravitational energy in the field which attracts them towards each other. When they are infinitely far apart, the gravitational attraction and hence energy approaches zero. As two such massive objects move towards each other, the motion accelerates under gravity causing an increase in the positive kinetic energy of the system. At the same time the gravitational attraction - and hence energy - also increase in magnitude. But the law of energy conservation requires that the net energy of the system does not change. This can only be resolved if the change in gravitational energy is negative, thus cancelling out the positive change in kinetic energy. Since the gravitational energy is getting stronger, this decrease can only mean that it is negative.[1]

       A universe in which positive energy dominates will eventually collapse in a "big crunch", while an "open" universe in which negative energy dominates will either expand indefinitely or eventually disintegrate in a "big rip". In the zero-energy universe model ("flat" or "Euclidean"), the total amount of energy in the universe is exactly zero: its amount of positive energy in the form of matter is exactly canceled out by its negative energy in the form of gravity.[2]

reformed, or cleansed energy, will effect us financially, as well as in every port, in such greater ways.

This phenomenon is true, being that our lives revolve around money. The more that this negative energy is removed, or transformed into a better structurally energetic formation, the greater the person's freedom in all scopes and expanses, in many areas of their life and not just in the space, or the sphere, where the negative energy was bound, which in this case, is in the monies formats to begin with, being that paper is not energetically in the positive energetic formats.

Let me reiterate. If we use our monies for any positive applications, we transform the negative parts of money into a positive energy force. If we utilize our finances for bad, we receive only negative in every part of the associations, or what we used that money for.

Since money is an Energic particle, no matter what you may currently think, you must be scrupulously "clean" and honest, in order to truly be happily successful. Meaning, honest with the charitable donations of tithings, as well as for the generosities of the creation processes, of the developments in our minds and manifesting greater ways of spending our earnings and thereby, creating such greater merchandise, or wares and micro-businesses and micro-niches and micro-products that serve humanities and thereby, create so much value and meaning in our lives and in the lives of many inhabitants and personalities, in our very better for you, having had monies in our world and therefore, the world rewards you by administering to you, so much more wealth and abundance.

Please, do not forget that the truer trick to creating wealth, is making sure that you are adding some value to our world. If you are just creating another "99 cents store", AKA common prototype, then you cannot expect to be successful. The energetically stimulated formulations of our world, will not let you be successful, no matter what, there is no value being added in your fabrication of your 99 cents store.

Again...
Please realize that, in order for truer successes, there needs to be an added value to our world, with your newer and innovatively better for our world inventory, or the success rate will be impeded upon you and be detrimental to you and our ways of our worlds economically sadder, right now world.

Cheating and stealing creates and distorts the energy into the energy of the lesser energetic formats and thereby, others will also, be able to steal from you in much greater and a larger scale formats. Usually, at the rate of three times what you stole.
Being that, this is just the beginning of another book in progress, called My Secret TextBook.

Please realize that, this is just the beginning and that these particles are so minutely and awe inspiring, that I had an avid need to explain this conceptual particles.

You see if we understand energy and thereby, make even small energetically positive changes, we can all have a better world, just by rejuvenating so many greater businesses, from our of the "Netherlands of bankruptcy", which is why I am writing this book, instead of finishing another just as greater book format.

It is important, to cultivate exactly that current, that is an abundance energetically greater particles of money. It is just a matter of tapping into that energy, and not hurting ourselves, by unknowingly utilizing the negative parts of energy, instead of the positive stimulating abundance formations of energy.

So, let us backtrack to our cash flow...
You see, if you "steal", or help oneself to, or secure monies, or funds from your business, for what ever reasons, or purposes...

Imagine..
By partaking, or just simply taking anything that is of these venues of cash, or aqueducts of giving out merchandise for free, or relinquishing inventory, or goods, at wholesale prices to the "Family Plan", as we talked about, or for these instructional purposes "stealing" from your own "cash flow", or any business financial parts, or any part of your business that is of value..

Please, really and truly individualize and masterly understand, that by securing from your business any financial, or inventory particles, you are in essence encroaching and sequestering and depleting and again, simply destroying your business and your abilities to procure and grow, so much more investments and interest on your monies.

You see, by not letting these inventories and cash flow, funnel and thereby, amplify and abound into the betterments and the expenditures, that are vitally necessary to stimulate and grow, a stabilized and "Founding Father's" type of business...

...the probabilities of, after a year's worth of taking from your till, or any particles of your inventory, or stock, you will be in the position of the negatively pressurized balances, of not being able to pay back the bills and the expenditures, that accumulated from the existing cash flow and from the original investments from your initial investment to procure your now, hopefully flourishing business.

You see, if you had an adequate investment to commence your business...

... and now, a year later, or two years later, or even six months later, you are again looking for an investor, or a "better interest rate" on your credit card, chances are that you instigated and retrieved and took in some formats, even in the slighter, or minute, or in the "barely there" ways of taking, either inventory, or monies from your cash flow, or simply, there is bound to be some formats of theft in your organization.

How do I explain and elucidate and paraphrase and reiterate and "rewind"...

In the analogy of "I can lead a horse to water to drink, but you can't make it drink"!!

I know that, is sounds in the overachiever formats of teaching...

But, if you are truly are in these formats of securing and partaking from your till, in any manner, or configuration, then you are in essence undermining and in the half hazard ways, truly stealing from your abilities and partaking of your adroitness of your competences and for sure futuristically extended and "Titanic" advancements..
How do I truly reiterate and expand and explicate, that this Formation of the "stealers wave length", will have so many more terrible "side effects" and in continuation..

..will extricate from your past expertise in your given field and of multifarious and multifold successes and thereby, the energetically greater "Formations" will put you in the energetically stimulated Tsunami sized, stealers wave length.

Trust me, I must expand on this phenomenon and thereby, please realize that, I am also, a greater ideologist of the varieties of many formations of energy..

You see, there are many variants, that are subject to evaluation and there are so many other obstacles in the energetic ways of monetary receivings..

Please realize that, the theft energetic stimulated energy, is like a Tsunami sized energetically greater components, with such greater and powerful energetic and physical stimulation, whereby, you have little, or no anchorage and no restraints, or control and are truly get swept away, not unlike a Tsunami...

You see, you are in the pathways, or the "eye of the storm", of the tornado and have no conation, or choice, but to be thieved and pilfered, from in every sectionate particles of your business..

You see, when this is the sadder case..

..imagine...
..even the shipping cost and not withstanding, even your favorite customer will abrogate and negate and not appreciate your time constraints. In the examples of missing appointments, or coming excruciatingly later than they should and thereby, the wastage of a calendar day of profits, that could have occurred with a different client. Even, an important business trip might have been postponed, for these alleged appointments.

..or, in the worse particles of this Formations of the Stealers and the energetically stimulated thievings of everything and anything that is "not cemented to the ground" and the abrogation of your retrievals, of so much more efforts than you are needed, to be putting into your livelihoods...

Please realize, that at this point in this time period, your well trusted employers will also, be skimming from your business, or your inventory, or any particles of your unknown and disorganized and unsystematic components of the entireties, of your cartel, or corporation, or the departments, or the jurisdiction that was entrusted to him and that they have imprimatur and certifications of managing and therefore, easily accessible.

You see, I know of this terrible story of this boss and his most trusted longer time period than most employee, that opened up his own store and utilizes the inventory that he poaches and pirates merchandise from his boss, in order to fill up his very greater store of inventory..

The worser parts of this story is that he also became a retailer and a wholesaler to accommodate his worser particles of thieving and misappropriating and pilfering funds, as well as for vendibles and payloads of containers, from imported parts of his bosses consignments and his many shiploads of wares..

Imagine, that for about twenty something years, no one knew about this terrible phenomenon and occurrence, or discerned of this impossibility of these kinds of proceedings of ever being possible...

This greater heist...

...until about a year ago and this was in continuance and believe it or not, going on for about thirty years and not counting any more...

Being, that he was finally outed!!

How do I explain this terrible phenomenon, or HAP to you?

The ways of this very stronger than normal energetical formation, is that in it's sad and scary parts of this "stealers formation", is that in this formation every proportionate parts of you and your lives are at risk and liability and exposed to being thieved and demoralized and embezzled and pilfered and peculated and misappropriated...

Imagine...
In every parts or components of your life... not solely in business!!

...your time periods and your talents and your physical beauty and health, are at risk and in peril and in jeopardy of being thieved at, as well as for any other segments and parts of your lives, of your spouse's life span and your very most important children's continuance, are in these very terrible energetically sadder compositions and formula.

Imagine..
..EVEN THOUGH THE MONEY IS YOURS!! You do not want to do this, trust me on that!

Yes!
I know...
... it is your business to take from, or draw evaluations and require and rely on and support your families with, or to do as you please!!

..or, you would think that...

But..
It is not about whose money, or funds, or inventory, it really belongs to.

Semantics, semantics...
But, energy is energy and we can not trick, or fool energy, ever.

We just need to be savvy and farsighted and perceptive and intelligent and understand the fundamentalities and the standardizations of the usages of energy, to our beneficial and the betterments of our well rounded lives..

I am here to undoubtedly and with a pure heart and conviction, tell you that at this point, you will be part of the tsunami sized, free radical energy field, that thinks that you are a thief and therefore, more of plagiarism, shop lifting, salespeople stealing and other terrible stealers formations, are parts of these energetical fields, as we talked about.

Like it, or not. These are the energy rules.

PLEASE REALIZE THAT WE NEED TO PUT AN ENED TO IT!!
Too many businesses are suffering.

The way to rid yourself, or eradicate these terribler energies, is to be as squeaky clean as humanly possible, in the formats of being honest and accounting for every single minutely inconsequential itemized particle of your business, that is relinquished and thereby, taken out of your business..

Please realize that, we will be needing to write everything down. Every penny, or inventory, or even a stapler, or a scotch tape dispenser, that is extricated from anywhere in your store, or business, needs to be accounted for.

Just write down everything!!!
Another possibility, is to just have a miscellaneous expense account, in addition to you salary and to take whatever you need, out of that account and consider it, as partialies parts of your salaries and wages.

You are then absolved and free from the responsibility of the stealer circle. You are exonerated and released and exulpated from a terrible financial burden.

Get ready to succeed in your business, in such an easier formats from here on!!

Chapter Three

Review

1. Please, elucidate and contrive, what "cash flow" truly mean?

_____
_____
_____
_____
_____
_____
_____
_____
_____
_____
_____
_____

2. Please tell me why cash flow is so important?

_____
_____
_____
_____
_____
_____
_____
_____
_____
_____
_____
_____
_____
_____

3. Please, give reason and instigate a plausible answer, to why you cannot navigate a business structure, without serious cash flows?

_____

_____

_____

_____

_____

_____

_____

_____

_____

_____

_____

_____

4. Please tell me of the misconceptions of cash flow equating to profits?

_____

_____

_____

_____

_____

_____

_____

_____

_____

_____

_____

_____

5. Please, paraphrase and define, what does EBITDA stand for and what expenses does it truly incur and inclusively incorporate?

_____

_____

_____

_____

_____

_____

_____

_____

_____

_____

_____

_____

6. Please, commentate and summarize, why it is so important to be scrupulously organized and honest, with your financial considerations, of doing your books?

_____

_____

_____

_____

_____

_____

_____

_____

_____

_____

7. Please, apprise and recapitulate, concerning the Cardinal sin of dispersing' of cash from your cash flow and pocketing, a few bills here and there?

_____

_____

_____

_____

_____

_____

_____

_____

_____

_____

_____

_____

_____

8. Please, epitomize and suggest, what is the recourse and what actions should be taken, if you need cash, or monies from your cash register?

_____

_____

_____

_____

_____

_____

_____

_____

_____

_____

_____

_____

9. Please, inform me and evince, what could occur in the negatively based parts if the cash flow is tampered with?

_____

_____

_____

_____

_____

_____

_____

_____

_____

_____

_____

_____

10. Please, define and establish, what a lien is and how does such a terrible phenomenon progress?

_____

_____

_____

_____

_____

_____

_____

_____

_____

_____

_____

11. Please, expand and epitomize, on how the energetically massive formats of stealing, come into the equation, even, when we disperse funds from our own businesses?

_____

_____

_____

_____

_____

_____

_____

_____

_____

_____

_____

12. Please, annotate and interject and expand, on how energy effects our business and our successes, of acquiring wealth and profitable revenues?

_____

_____

_____

_____

_____

_____

_____

_____

_____

_____

_____

_____

_____

_____

_____

_____

13. Please, interpose and reflect on how energetically, by adding value to our world with our product, or service and thereby, being that it is a needed commodity, the energy will masterly help you and the impending success of our business, or venue of receiving income, is in the for sure parts of the spectrums. Please, demonstrate a few examples.

_____

_____

_____

_____

_____

_____

_____

_____

_____

_____

_____

_____

14. Please, resolve and depict this conundrum of, are we truly thieving from ourselves, if we take monies, or petty cash from our tills and energetically we are stealing from ourselves? How can we alleviate this part of getting into the sadder formats of thieving from ourselves?

_____

_____

_____

_____

_____

_____

_____

_____

_____

_____

_____

15. Please, retort and denote, in the reciprocalities of taking from the till, energetically what truly could initiate and happen to a business?

_____

_____

_____

_____

_____

_____

_____

_____

_____

_____

_____

Chapter Four

The distinctions between Branding and
a Flagship Store or business...

What is the distinction and the antithesis and the contrast and of course, in a simpler formats the difference between Branding's and a Flagship store, or business?

When we utilize and appropriate the formats of a Flagship quality store, or in my case I have added and supplemented the abilities to also, further incorporate, or append a business, or a service oriented business, or volunteer, or free community services programs for schools, or synagogues, or a lithurgy for your Churches...

So, here are the most determining and existent and ponderous questions, to your "Branding" and "Flagship" parts of your lives..
Please, really individualize the differentiation between, how to articulate between what does it truly mean to "Brand" and what does it truly signify, to create an arête "Flagship" quality and of the higher calibration and of the standardized precipitation of, or structured Store, or business, or any structural venue even a service oriented, or volunteer outlet?

You see, the virtual understanding of Branding and of the Flagship terminology is that of the minor particles of getting their store outfitted, with more merchandise, which can create and actualize and constitute just, another "99cents store look alike"..

I alleviated these venues to understand and deduce these two differentiations, by pre-fabricating my own definition and my own interpretations, on what I imagine a "Flagship" configuration and better skeleton systematically morphology framework, should alway encompass and what a truer "Branding" structures and complex edifice should truly be composed of.

You see, Branding is just recognition and identification and remembrance and a format of "recall", just like the conceptual particles of the usages of "sight words", for pre-school children.

We basically, "train" our public to notice and diagnosticate and recollect a given product, or service by advertisements and by chants and by pictorials and by repetitive and aeolian and unvarying repetitive gestures, or "tools", like flash cards or other similar venues..

Please realize that, if done well, personifications of the given products, or services, or any venues that is being "Branded" actualizes, in the capacities of getting well known and becoming a house hold name, or a greater name brand, that has achieved the greater's of being a better proclamation of "why are we special"..

So, the "Branding's", is all about the name recognition and the actualizing of the understanding and the realization of this venue and the "getting to know you" of the product, or service, in the well known and the for sure parts of purchasing, or utilizing your service..

In the direct correlation and in parallelism and in similitude to our paragraphs that we talked about, in our recitation about "Oscar Meyer Weiner and Coca Cola".

So..

Now, let us talk about a truer Flagship style store, or business, or service, or any venue, in the restyling of what I would want the components of any Flagship to comprise and embody and incorporate..

First of all, please realize that, the norm of a Flagship is to have in this structure the abilities to connect, or interchange with merchandise..

..usually through computer systems and through available inventory, that is set and compiled into the structure of exaggerated supplies and in an overwhelmingly greater inventory for the "just in cases", that might happen and might not..

You see, the losses on these maybes, are always too much for any establishment to endure and equally more obstructive and destructive, than any possibilities of profits..

What I have elucidated here, is that these central, or primary and main stores, or these Flagship homogeneous type businesses, or Formations, are the central, or the Hub, or a conduit, or a channel, to the future identical name, and interchangeable and in the tantamount parts and in the exact same merchandise in different locals and the differentiations of countries..

Please, realize that another, mass parts of the initiation and the launching of a "Flagship" store, or the inception of any similar paradigm, or the commencement of a Flagship epitome service, or the birthing of any nonprofit Flagship genre, is for the sheer purpose of being the center...

... of your many nearer and further futuristically greater outlets, that you are hoping to create in the subsequent parts, of your soon to be greater and larger businesses..

Imagine, just having a "Flagship", just for the namesake and the "Branding" parts of being on the map of name brands and not just a "no name" business, or store, or venue of a service oriented production..

So.

You see again, the Flagship apparatus, or the "Hub" of your business, in every individually greater case, is the store or the forum, that is the advertisements and the endorsements and the crucial "broadcast station" and the venue of the promulgation of the name brand in question..

Please understand and truly individualize that each and every Flagship apparatus, must brave and experience and persevere and be in the branding parts and become recognized and well known and remarkable, to truly be a success story and positioned on the "map", that so to speak.

Ok.

We just in this parts of the discourse grasped the assimilation about the understandings and the comprehensions of what "Branding" is and a "Flagship" structure and configuration is, in the formats and framework and the skeleton framework, of the normal business discernment..

So, here goes my salutation of this subject matter and of course, this is just more of what we have been in precipitation of..

..What we have catechized and that we have expanded on already.

First of all..
You see, the difference between a Flagship store, or Flagship business, is akin and in analogous and likened to a rubber stamp.

Imagine, with just with the abilities to duplicate the impression and the imprint and the indentation of the stamp, as many times as you wish..

Imagine...then in the same formats for the creations and the genesis and the propagation and the birthing of many additional and appended stores, or supplementary businesses, or adjunct service oriented venues, or appurtenant community programs, or expanded Synagogues, or any subsequent structured formalities, of structural of any and all, mass parts of any financial institution.

You see, like I have stated before...in a different chapter..

If we are already in the process, or in the progression of going through the formalities and the trouble of the creations, or the Birthing's of a store, or the start-up of any modalities of business, or the inception of recreational facility, or the instigation of any religious ties, or the restructuring of any community centers, why not create them with the egg implanted in the structural parts, from the beginning..?

How much extra bother, or financial additional appended expenditures will it truly necessitate, to create this type of infra-structure that is already imbedded into the standardized structure, for the abilities of the future additional stores, or businesses, to grow without any greater "growing pains", from the birthing parts of the inceptions and the very genesis of any venture?

The answer is approximately 15%.

In this very simplified analogy, I hope to generate a better individualized comprehension on this ideology, of the "prep work" being in place for the nearer, or father futuristically accommodations of an easier growth, or upgrades, for the future particles of your venture.

Imagine, that you are renovating your home and your finances for now is budgeted..

The betters ways to renovate this home would be, if the finances are not there, let's say for example, for modernizing the attic..

Please realize that, the contractor will then at least prepare your attic with the pipping and the electrical wires in place, so that when the time comes to complete this tedious project, no wall will be needed to be broken and no walls will be needing to be repaired..

You see, in this ways of structuring...

The bathroom plumbing will be parallel and exactly on top of the floor underneath it, to facilitate an easier genesis of this attic. The kitchenette will have its gas pipping with an elbow to secure a preparation for the future oven, or gas range..

please realize that, the expert Contracter will then align the water pipes, in similarities and will be positioned in advance, with the architects help, to assure less future damage and thereby, less effort and expenses and more professionalisms in the near, or further futuristic parts..

Another beneficiallies, is the additions of more luxuries and more conveniences to this home, when he can more afford it.

In the exact replica of this understanding..

If we prepare every business structure to facilitate a Flagship... if every venue is in that structural qualities...

When we necessitate and are ardently ready for more..

You see, in the interim and in the interregnum of just having one Flagship constitution format of venue.. in the meantime, the worst scenario is..

The side effects are, just a better quality business..

Maybe, the expenditures of 15% more for the start up costs and the establishment and the inauguration of a new venue, if. Which we can utilize and luxuriate and appreciate, every particle now, of these structures..

Understandably, the business will have a greater computerized program and will be able to facilitate and expedite the tracking it's merchandise, with dates and time lines and chronicles of when the newer and next shipments are due to arrive and will be expected..

.. and with the infrastructure of having more organization and tabulation and Methodized structural parts, in order to better understand and discern, what is happening and every milestone and proceedings at every juncture of your business, so that you will be able to replicate and mimeo-reproduce this store, when the aspirations and when the financial infra-structure, will be able to accommodate the growth of another store, or location, of your venues.

I do not recommend, or advocate, or exhort, having extra storage for the facilitation, of more inventories..

I would rather have a styling and up-graded genre "walk in closet" not unlike the dry cleaners that posses an automatic systems in place, kind of structure, in a nearby location, so no transportation is necessitated..

Another, preeminent side benefit would be, the securing and the luxuries of less theft..

Not to forget, a better grasp on your business and no loose ends...

The know how of how much inventory you truly have and in what shape they are in, instead of the accumulation of too many goods because of dismemberment and disorganizations of your precious inventory, being that without it you have no business.

I would like to get you all, in every format of a business, or store, or service oriented structure, or community center, or synagogue to incorporate every individualize aspect of a Flagship quality structure, in order that each and every business, or venture, are interconnected and of a higher calibration and of the aspects of being able to interchange merchandise, or inventories, without the over buying and the over stockings...

Imagine, purchasing mass amounts of merchandise?..for the futile parts of the maybes, but with the profits being in that sedentary and just "sitting" inventory and collecting dust..

..and thereby, being able to collectively lose so much more, in the for sure parts, of using profits to just keep on purchasing inventory, for naught..

You see, we are needed to analyze and confab and assay and truly and individually understand, the differentiation and hydrolyze and philosophize, between a Flagship quality and of the higher calibration store formation and the Branding's of your idea, or product, or your service oriented businesses.

You see again, when we are initiating and we are inaugurating a new and preponderant business, or we are incorporating another "division", or demarcation, or a sectionate parts of your business, or rehabilitating your very antecedently more burdensome and harder and in the austere formats than the same normal venue, or just maybe, you are up-grading your established and concrete and existing performa, or just redecorating to spruce up and rejuvenate, your already quality day job..

Please realize that, we need to understand, that "Branding" is always needed to be successful...

No matter what. A rule, so to speak!

A Flagship performa, is in the analogous parts, of just having the egg inside that very first store, or first restructuring of your fossil like and tired business...

..and therefore, an easier birthing, or re-birthing, of your second and third and fourth...stores and thereby, considerably preferably exceptionally superior cohesiveness and greater NET profits.

So, just to reiterate..
What does it mean to "Brand"?

"Branding" means that our product becomes well know and predictable. We basically know what we are purchasing. No surprises.

In "Branding" we must preserve the product by keeping it consistent and therefore, the same and coequal of the product will be the selling point.

Anything and everything can be marketed and sold therefore, they need to be "Branded", first and foremost for recognition.

I already explained "Branding", further on with an actress. If she, or he is predictable, then when they have a part that fits them, then it is an easy "Shidduch", or union, for the two actors to mesh.

You see, in ever parts of our business world, the biggest expense that concur and has permeated our businesses, in such greater proportionately greater parts, is the "Branding's" of our products.

My goal it to create profits with ease, by stimulating our business and by injecting and infiltrating our business with the natural Branding parts, already infused in the namesake of our business, or stores, or any parts of earning a living.

By including and by accommodating in the process of writing this book, I have started writing this book, with the egg inside the thought processes of writing this book, from the go..

Just from the title.

Because, I have taken a name that was a conceptual particle and a philosophically greater parts of many conversations, it is a shoe in, when it comes to "Branding" acknowledgments.

You see, we all have heard and rustled an agitated conversation, of "what came first the Chicken, or the egg.

Title recognition at its finest...
(A form of piggy backing, as we will be talking about it)

Imagine, for over eighty years and counting, we just went in circles trying to understand the answer to our timeless question, of what came first the chicken, or the egg?

One more time:
Please realize that "Branding" is about creating consistencies, so that when you purchase your item, the expectations are on target and in the realm of exactly, what you wanted and expected.

Please realize that, when it came to "Branding" my book, I just "piggy backed" on the past Branding's of over 85 years, of the conceptual parts, of *What came first the chicken or the egg?*

By, me "Branding" my book, imagine, just with the name and therefore, the possibilities and the opportunities of creating and actualizing a "Flagship type Book", are great. Maybe, I could bring into existence a Flagship for the authorship Deborah Shaul.

Yes, yes, I know that it's tenor sounds, "a little out there." But, please, under any condition and every condition, try to Brand your business, or book, or any parts of your instituting in the form of selling, or marketing something.

You see, I was "Branding" my book and my name sake, at the very genesis and `beginning of the creation process, of my book. Even, before the thought process...

I started with the name. Please realize that, every book thereafter that has this name..
...as book one, or book two, or book three, already is an easier sell and the egg, that was already implanted in my book, is ready to hatch.

Name recognition!

You heard the words before. It is not new to you!!
What came first the chicken or the egg?
You do not have to start from scratch, for people to remember this question.

I philosophically academically and expertised early on and retrieved lessons from God's creation process. I, thought about the future, at the inquest and at the genesis and first minutes of writing this book.

Just, like God did.

When, we already conversed and had our discourse and discussed how God created the chicken, with the egg already implanted inside the chicken, primed and I readiness and ready to hatch and begin and substantiate and commence, another supplementary generation of chickens..

You see... so, that the future is fed with ease and of course, us not messing up God's very greater creations and cooking the egg, before it hatches and not, realizing that Southern Fried Chicken was on the menu, also.

How do I explain to you that I am by nature an analogyst and therefore, I will explain that any business can have the "Branding" qualities, implanted in the very core of your structural parts of your business...

Yes.
Already, in it's structure of any business, or store formats, or any venue, of earning a living, just like our God created the chicken with the egg already implanted and inside the chicken.

Please realize that, it is God's nature, to always realize the future in it's original fruit, and to always think and tribulate and create, the future parts at the beginning of any portionate parts of our creations.

You see, because God takes great satisfaction in giving unconditionally and assuring us, that we are secure in the future and in this case our protein particles of our menus and our edible parts of making sure, that every parts of our programs are never endangered to alleviate the food structures.

You see again, the apple and the avocado and the grapes and the olives and almost every fruit, has it's seeds already implanted in it's very greater fruit. From before these fruit even ripened!!

We must necessitate and be committed to doing the same with any idea, or product, any business venture, that we put into play, or create...

The natural progression of the ways of our world, of contemplating and of obscuring the after parties of the after world's and the after gratuitous and the inspired ways of the future in every entireties of every portionate parts, that God had ever created and therefore, the successful way of creating anything, or any venture that we would want to produce, or even to reformat, into another upgraded version, of what was, is to imitate our God.

If you still have issues with this conceptual particles, how do I understand the notion and hypothesis pertaining to me, in the the formats of the chicken with the egg implanted in its womb?

What does this greater concept, have to do with my ideology and "Branding" and creating a Flagship quality store?

Please, let me explain to you the P's and the Q's, of truly opening up a "Branded" Flagship store.

You see, at the conception, or the true Genesis of a store, or a business, meaning even just at the thought process of opening up a store, or a business...

At the higher calibration energetical parts of creation and therefore, in the most lucrative time of instilling and implanting, anything and everything, that we designate and therefore, choose to elevate and succeed and triumph.

This conceivably and perchance could be our business, or perhaps our store, or imaginable, even "Branding" of our selves.

Please understand that, when you expedite opening up your first store, or the inception of a first business. If you initiate the dawn of any venue, with the thought process of this store, or business, it will be so much greater and preponderant.

What impediments would I add in a store, in preparation for the flagship quality and organization parts?

If I am creating a store, or a business, I would make sure that I have instill and impregnate and intermix a more advanced computer program, as well as, a much more robust and stalwart and sturdy and concrete established institution and organized infrastructure.

In a mandatory venue, I would have a better Website. I would even build a Website with the futuristic abilities, of having abundant and plenteous pages and search engines that have the aptitude of having the dexterity and the performa and comprehension of my up-grading my website, or any parts of it.

I endorse, loyal employees that gain percentages of future NET Profits..

..it is in my opinion mandatory...
A natural, and a "shoe in" for loyalty and continuance, for our most important moving pieces, our workers being gratified and therefore, do a better performa in their employments mass particles.

I would engineer my business with the framework and the invent and the capacities capabilities to interconnect, with computerized configurations and elaborately sophisticated phone systems, with the abilities to commission plentiful persons, without much ado.

With a future Flagship quality and superiority infrastructure store, or business **in mind,** commissioning's and securing a position for this new store job title, or business, needs to be a conscious and a concise decision.

You see, this parts of the hiring, or this parts of implanting the egg inside the chicken, the future seed inside the business of the future...

This well perceived and very robustly thought out and truly individualize and contemplated, as if you are truly hiring them for this better, or esteemed job opportunity, of being in a Flagship quality Business, or store.

You see, if they would be the best employee in that given field, if your store became a vast up-graded Flagship store, instead of a worker for a smaller and less busy store, or business that are smaller and inferior in structural quality, **that is the indicator of whether you are implanting the seed inside the business, not unlike the egg in the chicken, at the go.**

You see, with a newbie business, you can not start with less quality employees at the beginning. With a greater ease, you can hire more new employees, later on, by making sure that there is a place and a talent, for each employee from the conceptual parts, of the starting of your business.

Please realize that, one of the most fundamentally important segments, that I truly aspire to and equally long for and truly individualize for and desideratum in such greater ways, that you all will not disremember at the inception of the creation process, or modus operandi of your business, or onset of your store, is the "Branding".

I am sure, that all of you have heard and perceived of "Branding" so, let me explain and expand and analyze a minute portionate parts about it, so you will comprehend and envisage, that "Branding" needs to be engaged and committed and in a greater performance and in "all systems go", in order to have a Flagship quality business, in pursuit and thereby, in play.

First of all, "Branding" is a process that is usually done by professionals, but I will try and teach you all, how to have a natural components to "Branding," which means that, we will infuse our "Branding's" in the Beginning conceptions of our business and have the egg inside the chicken metaphorically, ready to hatch.

Branding means that, like *"Oscar Meyer Weiner's"* advertisement, that we all know so well, or [9]*"hold your pickles hold your lettuce, special orders don't upset us, all we ask is that you have it your way, at Berger King."* We cognize and mimic these repetitive recurrent sing-song advertisements easily.

These foods are automatically identified!

You see, these two advertisements were done well and they were meant to "Brand" and they did the job. I imagine, it cost them over a half a Billion dollars to get that famous.

First of all, what does it mean to "Brand" well?

To "Brand" well, means that they have repeated and recapitulated in perpetum the same advertisements consistently and thereby, there is **name recognition.**

I truly want to teach you all, to have your "Branding" abilities in your name sake, or appellation of your business, or

---

[9]   Burger King was launched in 1954 in Miami by James McLamore and David Edgerton as a fast-food restaurant with indoor dining. The "Whopper" sandwich was introduced in 1957, and Hume, Smith & Mickelberry first advertised the restaurant as "Home of the Whopper" in local TV spots in 1958.

venue, so that we won't need to purchase advertisement space, of over a half a billion, to become that well known.

So here are a few rules.

1. Always place and assign the product that you are selling, as the first word in your name sake of your business.

For example, I have a wig business, so I name it "Wigs by Deborah". Not Deborah Wigs. The wigs needed to be placed and installed in the first word, because of a few important reasons, including "Branding".

You see, in every Google-like **search engine** your business, with your niche products first word in your title, will come up close to first.

Another positive, is that no one will have to guess what you are selling. It is clear and concise and with a greater **clarity of what your inventory** consist of.

How many of us have scrolled many businesses, being that we were in quandary and we were hesitant and we were simply unsure about the true classifications, of the product being sought after?

2. Another, important parts of "Branding" is a **logo picture type**, or emblem, or creating an insignia that also tells the viewer, our public what we are selling, with certainty and clarity and decipherabilities.

3. Another important things with "Branding" is being very **CONSISTENT**. Invariable with packaging. Homogeneous with the product. Uniform with advertising. Our patrons do not want to guess our product over and over.

Our patrons necessitate predictability. Expected and consistency is the higher level of Branding.

You see, when a client gains entrée into your show room, or store, they want consistency and accountabilities with ease and similarities.

Our patrons require, spending as limited time as possible looking for things.

Similarly to Duane Reed, where no matter which replication of a store you entered into, they are almost identical and thereby, easier to find every conceivably minute object and thereby, purchase with ease from these same kinds of stores.

4. Another important aspect of "Branding", is to get your name sake visually and visibly and ocularly seen and noticed.

You see, there might be the necessities of purchasing advertising space, in many different venues..

Please realize that, the most common utilized ones are not necessarily the right ones for your business..

You see again, if you own a wholesale company that markets. or contracts, of any forms of school supplies, for instance..

The logical venue would be, to locate near a school, but or a University..

The vitally important and determining parts are, is to think and envisage and calculate and predict, in terms of demand equates to supply and without a greater venue of demand, your supply with just "create dust", so to speak, or God forbid, end up in some retail stores detrimental and of greater losses of revenues and profits, "Sales Rack".

By truly creating a greater "Branding" product, or store, or service oriented business, you are assured of the "traffic" and the better parts of the certainties, that your "Brand" attracts the perfect Avatar and the perfect clientele, or customers and patrons, that will not only appreciate your better inventory, but will for certain be return patrons and tell their very greater friends, that are in the "Like attracts Like" categories, that will most probably also, be a greater consumer of your very market, that you are marketing and that you are "Branding".

Chapter Four

Review

1. Please, illustrate and reveal in detail and as many features and amenities that you can conceivably think up, concerning the instigating of the commencements of a greater
1. Flagship Store.

_____
_____
_____
_____
_____
_____
_____
_____
_____
_____
_____
_____
_____
_____
_____
_____
_____
_____
_____
_____
_____
_____
_____
_____

2. Wholesale business.

3. Tutor

4. Lawyers practice

5. Dental hygienist

6. Contractor

7. Actor/singer?

_____

_____

_____

_____

_____

_____

_____

_____

_____

_____

2. Please, itemize as many features and amenities, that you can conceivably think up concerning the instigating of the commencements of an esteemed Branding programmation?

   1. Store?

_____

_____

_____

_____

_____

_____

_____

_____

_____

_____

_____

_____

_____

_____

_____

2. Wholesale business?

_____

_____

_____

_____

_____

_____

_____

_____

_____

_____

_____

_____

_____

_____

_____

_____

Tutor?

_____

_____

_____

_____

_____

_____

_____

_____

_____

_____

_____

_____

_____

_____

_____

_____

_____

_____

_____

_____

_____

_____

_____

_____

_____

_____

_____

_____

_____

_____

3. Lawyers practice

_____

_____

_____

_____

_____

_____

_____

_____

_____

_____

_____

_____

_____

_____

_____

_____

_____

_____

_____

_____

_____

_____

_____

4. Dental hygienist?

_____

_____

_____

_____

_____

_____

_____

_____

_____

5. Contractor?

_____

_____

_____

_____

_____

_____

_____

_____

_____

_____

_____

_____

_____

_____

_____

_____

_____

_____

6. Actor/singer?

_____

_____

_____

_____

_____

_____

_____

_____

_____

_____

_____

_____

_____

_____

_____

_____

_____

_____

_____

_____

_____

_____

_____

_____

_____

_____

_____

3. Please tell me why the name sake is so important?

_____

_____

_____

_____

_____

_____

_____

_____

_____
_____
_____
_____
_____
_____
_____
_____
_____
_____
_____
_____
_____
_____
_____
_____
_____
_____
_____
_____
_____
_____

4. Please tell me the formats that these companies utilized for their very Branding parts and do you agree with what they did.. in the ways that we learned what would you do differently?

1. Coca Cola

_____
_____
_____
_____
_____

2. Oscar Meyer Weiner

5. Please, instigate and therefore masterly commence a Flagship Quality structure, for each one of these formats of reciprocations of receiving monetary compensations?
   1. Synagogue?

   _____

   _____

   _____

   _____

   _____

   _____

   _____

   _____

   _____

   _____

   _____

   _____

   _____

   _____

   _____

   _____

   _____

   _____

   _____

   _____

   _____

   _____

   _____

   _____

2. Community Center?

_____

_____

_____

_____

_____

_____

_____

_____

_____

_____

_____

_____

_____

_____

_____

_____

_____

_____

_____

_____

_____

_____

_____

_____

_____

_____

_____

3. Online business?

6. Please, break down and articulate the extra cost, that would incur by creating a Flagship Quality store, or business, or any monetary venue, as opposed to the normal formats of creating a store, or a business?

_____
_____
_____
_____
_____
_____
_____
_____
_____
_____
_____
_____
_____
_____
_____
_____
_____
_____
_____
_____
_____
_____
_____
_____
_____

7. Please, epitomize and substantiate what classifications of employees do you employ for a a Flagship Quality store, or business, or any monetary structure of receiving monies? Please, itemize a list.

_____
_____
_____
_____
_____
_____
_____
_____
_____
_____
_____
_____
_____
_____
_____
_____
_____
_____
_____
_____
_____
_____
_____
_____
_____
_____

8. Please certify and conclude, that In the Flagship Quality store, or business module, what is the fundamentally of the most importance, to acquire greater customer service and customer satisfaction?

_____

_____

_____

_____

_____

_____

_____

_____

_____

_____

_____

_____

_____

_____

_____

_____

_____

_____

_____

_____

_____

_____

_____

Chapter Five

Creating the infrastructure of the Flagship quality Stores or Businesses.

The phenomenon, that I am trying to implicate in this chapter, and in plain English..is that if you are already opening up a business, or a store, or a service oriented business, with any monitory structure involved, meaning Capital, or even a volunteer structure, or a public service...

Ok.
If you are going through the hardship and the long hall and the travail and the educationally preeminent formats of becoming an esteemed teacher, or an expert Doctor, or an artistically inclined Dentist, or an astuter Businessman, or woman..

If you are truly ready to create and commence and inaugurate and open up a structured business..

Why not institute and restructure and augment a business, that has the structure of a Flagship quality store, already implanted, likened to the metaphorical egg, that is already being nurtured in the womb, so to speak, of the chicken?

You might as well..

You see, the financials are close enough..
Like I said.. maybe another 15% additional capital would be needed, but, it is so minor in this point, in any business structure.

How could you not realize that, there is the potentials and the abilities of maybe, even you structuring a Flagship, at minute higher costs and time lines, with just the formats and the infrastructure in place, for the futuristically greater needs of better computerized programs and increased additional qualified employees and larger augmented space, or aggrandized micro-niche inventories..

You see, if you do not end up creating more stores... and thereby, you just have this one better quality store, with the egg already implanted inside the chicken, so to speak.. you might as well.

That is the worst scenario.. imagine that!!

So, here we go.
Please realize that, there are a few fundamental rules for opening these kind of stores..

Imagine, in this analogy of construction.. pipe work in your kitchen and you are thinking that you might have a barbecue added, at some point in time...

The structure, that you would put the gas pipes, would be to add extra pipping in the wall and possibly an outlet, so that when you purchase that barbecue, all you have to do is purchase a further attachment for the pipe, to facilitate attaching the nozzle of the pipping of the new barbecue.

Imagine then, if I would not have prepared for the barbecue in advance,

Then, I would have had to break walls and possibly, put in new tile work and different flooring..

You see, the renovations and construction job, would have been that much more extensive and expensive, instead of the easier route, of having all the "prep work" being concluded and consummated in advance.

If you strategize in contrivance in the beginning, when there were no walls, or floors, the facilitation of executing and perfecting these regulations and procedures, would be much easier and much more inexpensive.
Any additions are easily added and are easily acclimated to our budget, as well as for the eco friendly particles of getting things done, without hurting the business and "doing business as usual", even with minor repairs being done at the same time.

Please realize that, in order to create and facilitate and to expedite an excelling Flagship quality store, or business, we require and we warrant and **must** create and design and fabricate it, at the truer first parts of creating and the "birthing" parts and in the conceptional mass parts, of our soon to be birthed, greater business.

Let me explain and elucidate and disclose to all of you, what a Flagship Store, or business methodologies and what ingredients and what constituencies and fundamentallities and components truly pertain to us, in our flagship's fabrications and edifice and the greater particles of the constructions and even the pre-birthing and the pre-conceivably producing's and developing's, of the egg this time around..

Imagine, thereby, rebirthing while still in the incubation periods, while still incubating inside the chicken, so to speak, while still in the "start up" parts of our business, or our store.

With this analogy in mind, please realize that a "Flagship" is a "prototype" store, or a vessel-like business, utilized and used in the application like the "commanding post" as the one outstanding and considerably preeminently larger, or greater store, or businesses, that images prototypes, **not unlike using a stamp, to create a duplicate image.**

My aspiration is to create each store, or business, in replication and in the magnitude of the original "Flagship" Store and thereby, each store is designed with the abilities and the qualities, of being in the exactness of the original prefabricated and with upgrading abilities, in it's original constitution and designing's of your original first "Flagship" Store, or Business.

Exactly like a "Model Home" in a development..

You see, it is necessary for the "Flagship" store, or business, that will be the "Commanding Post" metaphorically, to have many components and designs..

You see, in order for the "Flagship" to be able to have many sister stores, or twin stores and thereby, be viable as a Flagship component and a "role model", for what a store **must** look like and what variables and what modalities and it's entireties of it's structures must obtain..

Please realize that, in order to aspire equalities and growth and evolution and proliferation in each and every store, whether it is just in our Country, or around the Globe, these factors are mandatory and vital and a prerequisite.

In order to truly elevate and expand and advance and of course multiply and with constant duplicities for any store, or business, there needs to have many components;

I would like to organize and catalogue our thought processes and analyze and review, how to truly create a "Flagship" quality structure, at the start and at the onset and by the inception of the creation process of our store, or business.

Please realize that the store, or the business has to have these decisive and essential issued parts, in order to shift and to be able to transform and metamorphose the store, or business, into a "Flagship" constitution quality venue.

The "Flagship" style store, or business needs to have the ability to imitate and to duplicate and echo and literally "clone", every aspect of the store, or business, easily..

..Exactly like that rubber stamp, that we talked about.

In order to "clone" and in order to replicate and "carbon copy" every integral component and every fundamentally important fraction, of every module of every parts of the business, these points that we will be studying and analyzing, will guide and be a compendium to you, in similarities to the abc's, of how to plan ahead for a "Flagship" store, or business or any Merchandary venue.

1. The first most important "ingredient", is thinking in a grandeur and in an exaggerated format, as if you have already succeeded.

In the very beginning of developing our store, or business we must **"think big"** in copious amounts, even if the funds are not there. Everything, must be done in a greater organized way and in the preparations of the totalities, of your very greatest successes possible, for that particular business.

What does thinking big truly and in an individualist point of view, of each and every infrastructure, of any formats of any business truly equate to?

What does thinking in a prodigious and mammoth and in a copious manner and in a big way, truly signify and adumbrate, to you as a greater personality in reassessing, or launching and birthing and in the beginning particles of the "Genesis" of your store, or business opportunements?

One of the most important parts of "thinking big", or intellectualizing in a colossal grandeur ways of visualizing on a much grandiose and monumental scale and thereby, you are primed and "all systems go" for success..

Amongst these formats of thinking in the grandeur venues, is the expectation of the circulation of the abundantly masterfully patrons and return customers..

..with the expectations of the growth of your venue in greater proportions, in a faster ways and therefore, the necessities to prepare for the growth of your business, or venue, is in the the beginnings and in the Genesis parts, of birthing of your businesses..

You have in the "for sure parts" thereby, allotted and apportioned amount of monies aside for hiring extra personnel, before the need, or their requirements, of their services.

This very important particle of the creation processes of a truer Flagship quality business, or store, is that we must allocate room for employees and imagine that we are going to be that successful and that busy.

Another vital factor and is in the formats of the fundamentalities, is an even greater and upgraded computer program and systemized formats, for the enhancements of every single particles of every sectionate, or module and categories of every moving parts and stationary systems of every category of necessities of any structured venue, or business, or service oriented program of monetary value, or even, in the formats of being socially adept or volunteer or of a comunity service.

Being, that this is just he beginning of many important parts of being a quality and an enhanced personnel for this very structure of this personification of me being the arbitrator and thereby, I will be the one to complete this parts by my self because our have erred in many ways with your own formats of the creations of a flagship quality store and evaluation and inventory and customer satisfaction. Patron gratification, simultaneously for their voice being heard, in what their greater needs are compulsory and imperious.

We must and I mean must, in person coupled with on line programs, receive feedback and their "Aladdin's Lamp" of what they wish and dream of purchasing.

Please realize that, these parts are in the necessary and mandatory parts of the growth and the aggrandizement and the cultivations and prosperity and in the nearer futuristically multiplications, of farther and boundless added Flagship quality businesses, or store formations.

You see, by allocating many employees, mostly in part time positions to start, so that in the nearer future, when putting these newer persons and programs in place, with many greater of high ranking positions, they will easily glide and lubricate into place, with the simplicity and the actualities of a "Time Warner Nationally Acclaimed Movie".

You see, again, if you have already trained employees, when the need for a greater formats of help is sequestered, your business will have that "booster shot" on "automatic feed", to renegade and to truly elevate and thereby, create a well lubricated Flagship quality structure, that can easily be replicated.

These "models" and these greater, can easily be duplicated and can easily create replicas, or sister stores, all over the Country and then all over the Universillies, just like a rubber stamp, that can easily replicate an exact image instantaneously, and in perfection of being in the same gratis performa.

Please realize that this example is of
In this example and in this experience of mine, many years ago and in this future prototype, this is one of the "target practice" of successes, in the ways that I thought "big" and in the ways of starting out without funds or without the financial support of a larger scale operation.

You see, I opened up a company and a factory in my dining area. The size of this "room", was about 10 square feet, if.

I hired ten professional personnel and started training them in, at a stronger and more formatted structures, of imagining that our company was in "full shuttle cruise control evaluation", as well as in the fullest service possible, minus the pay was smaller and minimal, as is the case in newer "start ups".

By now, I already hired the personal secretary, as well as all of the factory workers, that I would have needed to hire when my orders came in, in the busier seasons, as well as in the granting's of the "Aladdin Lamp" and being that it was "just" an up-grading from an older business, that I have been involved in and considerably successful at.

I could have managed easily, at these beginner stages, in this business forum with about 2-3 workers, or employees, at this juncture. I was just in the restructuring and up-grading particles of a very successful basement business and thereby, "re-jump-starting" my business, in similarities to a "booster shot".

Please realize that, I already had a business, but it is always important to me to metamorphose and to revolutionize my business every year and I was at that very point of needing to up-grade, being that at this point in time, it was approximately 15 years into my business and counting. Now, I have completed and concluded over 34 years, in the same business and counting.

You see, in likened to most successful businesses, I did indeed upgrade in some fashionistà formats every year and maybe, even every bi-yearly, as I have mentioned is a must!!.

Ok.

So, in this exercise, it would perceivably be suggestive, that I contracted too many Staff members and the implications suggest, that I chartered too many faculty members and the insinuations theorize, that I enlisted too many professional artisans and that in simpler and plainer ways of saying, hired too many workers, in the now, to accommodate the nearer futuristically greater sales and productions.

You see, in order to have a truly lubricated business, meaning easier flowing business structure, without any impediments, or"road block" so to speak...

If the finances are not as bountiful...

Please, just hire as many people as you will desideratum and thereby, need in the imminent future and start these greater personnel commissioned and working, even once or twice weekly.

Please realize that, we are in dire essential demand and requisite, to not only facilitate our employees "training in" time period, but to masterly ameliorate and ease and condition their work ethics and integrate their greater proness and proficiencies, so that when you are God willing, "imploding at the seams" and "raking in the monies', you are in a time period of ease and know how and in the formulation of "bring it on" and not in anyway a panic mode, which will deter and allay and disburse and of course, chase away any greater purchaser, or higher grade savvy client, or a preeminent consumer.

But in the reality, by having so many prodigious and outstanding employees, I reaped in the rewards and the benefits of the commercially remunerative financial successes. I was also, by the way, instrumental in jump starting a more modernized programmations and "plan of action" and computerized systematically contendingly alabaster and retrograde, renovated product. I masterly renewed energetically greater particles of energy and revamped and up-graded an already growing business.

It not only paid off, but, I received so many newer orders and clients and customers, for my efforts.

Why?

Because, first of all I introduced a new and beyond what was out there in the market.

Back to my teachings, of the "Must Haves" of the micro-niche..

But, in the framework of their price budget and in the frame work of their standardized inventory, that my customers would be familiar with..

Yes, a micro-niche product that was in the exactness of performa, that my customers would have dreamed of purchasing and in the sameness of the quality and their price budget, even though this newer design was approximately $2,000 higher, in the evaluation of their cost effective parts, of being a fashionistá woman and thereby, the price was never an issue.

I just want to add in here, that I made the cardinal misstep and the death of my business, by going on sale out of fear of a slower than normal season and then, the price was always a problem and the bargaining was nauseatingly tiresome. I attracted the "bottom feeders" of the market...

Ugh!!

Another particle of hiring and commissioning too many personnel, at the beginning of any venture, is that I had everything in place for top performance.

You see, instead of waiting on line for a half hour or more, we were able to accommodate and in the convenience and in the funner and in the easements of our dedicated and loyal and appreciated clients, of their burdens of shopping, into a well lubricated portionate parts of running a smooth business, with a greater customer service base and without the altercations, of "things falling through the cracks", so to speak.

By truly being ready and primed and equipped and in the "all hands on deck" modes of doing business and in the formats of having everything in place and ready for greatness...

That is why success happens in the forefront of any greater opportunities, that come our ways.

The next parts of creating a solid foundation and a quality structure of a better Flagship store or business...

You must by now realize that, I thought in a grandeur ways of achieving's and creating many formats of advertisements, of free give aways and business cards and web sights and many other formats of increasing and extending and growing my business.

I created a systematically greater via paper, unfortunately in retrospect and in hindsight, that was not the way of the importuned, or the mega business modalities. I then needed to truly order a computer program in the eleventh hour, at about $100,000, but without the funds,

I created the programmations instead on paper, soon to be orchestrated in the better ways of the computer age.

How do I explain to you, that the most important parts of this instructional, in the creation of a Flagship quality business, or store, is that you are needed to be ready for the uptake and the ascendancy and the éclat ways of your successes of your business.

You see, at that point in time, you do not have to turn away business, because of the unavailabilities and the infrastructure, of not being able to accommodate a larger amount of, for me, custom orders on wigs, and in a timely manner..

Let us not make a misrepresentation, of what I am trying to express in the last paragraph...

Overstocking and over buying is the biggest blunder of any company, or store..
The profits thereby, are in the inventory and not in your bank account, or in your further investments.

What are the connotations, in the discrepancies of what I am writing?

Over buying means listening and being cajoled by the Chinese factories and purchasing 10,000 of each color, or style to receive a discount, or even a lesser amount.

Please realize that, even if you are a mega corporation, the chances that you are taking with each dollar value, of doing the easier and commodious and facile route of doing a preponderantly undemanding transaction..

Imagine...
On a larger scale business. Ordering the same merchandise in six colorations, or in every size group, is detrimental to your now and future flourishing's and ameliorations, of your businesses.

In this crazier story..
I had a friend that purchased 100,000 dresses, that were the exact replications and in the exactness and repeat sizings.

Now..
We have a population, in the category of women that would wear that particular style and sizing in New York, where he was only selling this merchandise in, at about 500 persons, if.

What are the chances of having 100,000 women with the same exact sizing and the same exact dress in the same exact colorations?

Now.
Please realize that, even if the number would have been much larger at 5,000 women, or 10,000...

Do you see us women wearing the exact same dress and thereby, be wearing a standardized uniform?

Do you imagine, that 5,000 women would be wanting to wear that exact same dress and most probably, be at the same functions, or in the same work places, being that New York is such a smaller State, than anyone truly individualizes, or realizes..? My friend, was correct in purchasing the large amount of[10]inventory, in order to

---

[10]   Inventory Wikipedia
    For the 1989 Polish film, see Inventory (film). For ecological inventory, see Forest inventory.
    Electronics inventory.
    Inventory or stock refers to the goods and materials that a business holds for the ultimate purpose of resale (or repair).[nb 1]
    Inventory management is a science primarily about specifying the shape and placement of stocked goods. It is required at different locations within a facility or within many locations of a supply network to precede the regular and planned course of production and stock of materials.
    The scope of inventory management concerns the fine lines between replenishment lead time, carrying costs of inventory, asset management, inventory forecasting, inventory valuation, inventory visibility, future inventory price forecasting, physical inventory, available physical space, quality management, replenishment, returns and defective goods, and demand forecasting. Balancing these competing requirements leads to optimal inventory levels, which is an ongoing process as the business needs shift and react to the wider environment.
    Inventory management involves a retailer seeking to acquire and maintain a proper merchandise assortment while ordering, shipping, handling and related costs are kept in check. It also involves systems and processes that identify inventory requirements, set targets, provide replenishment techniques, report actual and projected inventory status and handle all functions related to the tracking and management of material. This would include the monitoring of material moved into and out of stockroom locations and the reconciling of the inventory balances. It also may include ABC analysis, lot tracking, cycle counting support, etc. Management of the inventories, with the primary objective of determining/controlling stock levels within the physical distribution system, functions to balance the need for

achieve a greater portionate parts of the [11]profit margins,

---

product availability against the need for minimizing stock holding and handling costs.

[11] EditWatch this pageRead in another language Wikipedia
Profit margin
Profit margin, net margin, net profit margin or net profit ratio is a measure of profitability. It is calculated by finding the net profit as a percentage of the revenue.[1]

net profit margin

=

net profit
revenue
$\text{net profit margin}=\frac{\text{net profit}}{\text{revenue}}$
Net profit is revenue minus cost.

Profit margin is calculated with selling price (or revenue) taken as base times 100. It is the percentage of selling price that is turned into profit, whereas "profit percentage" or "markup" is the percentage of cost price that one gets as profit on top of cost price. While selling something one should know what percentage of profit one will get on a particular investment, so companies calculate profit percentage to find the ratio of profit to cost.

The profit margin is used mostly for internal comparison. It is difficult to accurately compare the net profit ratio for different entities. Individual businesses' operating and financing arrangements vary so much that different entities are bound to have different levels of expenditure, so that comparison of one with another can have little meaning. A low profit margin indicates a low margin of safety: higher risk that a decline in sales will erase profits and result in a net loss, or a negative margin.

Profit margin is an indicator of a company's pricing strategies and how well it controls costs. Differences in competitive strategy and product mix cause the profit margin to vary among different companies.[2]

Profit percentage   Edit

On the other hand, profit percentage is calculated with cost price taken as base and therefore, looking for the best price for his inventory..

You see, he thought, that if he could get a better [12]price point, which is necessary for his future, or already existing

---

profit percentage

=

net profit
cost price

*

100
%

$${\displaystyle {\text{profit percentage}}={{\text{net profit}} \over {\text{cost price}}}*100\%}$$

Suppose that something is bought for $50 and sold for $100.

Cost price = $50
Selling price (revenue) = $100
Profit = $100 − $50 = $50
Profit percentage (profit divided by cost) = $50/$50 = 100%
Return on investment multiple = $50 / $50 (profit divided by cost).
If the revenue is the same as your cost, profit percentage is 0%. The result above or below 100% can be calculated as the percentage of return on investment. In this example, the return on investment is a multiple of 0.5 of the investment, resulting in a 50% gain.

[12] Price point Wikipedia
Page issues

Price points A, B, and C, along a demand curve (where P is price and Q represents demand)
Price points are prices at which demand for a given product is supposed to stay relatively high.

Contents
Characteristics   Edit

Introductory microeconomics depicts a demand curve as downward-sloping to the right and either linear or gently convex to the origin. The downwards slope generally holds, but the model of the curve is only clients, then his profits are in the "for sure sales" parts of his business. Not.

He ended up, with loses just on this minor for him, transaction about $5,000,000 in junk inventory and in 99 cents of qualities of dresses.

Ugh for him!!

Ok.

For the clarifications and for the esteemed particles of truly inaugurating and discerning and understandings, in the better and simplistically obvious formats...

---

piecewise true, as price surveys indicate that demand for a product is not a linear function of its price and not even a smooth function. Demand curves resemble a series of waves rather than a straight line. [citation needed]

The diagram shows price points at the points labeled A, B, and C. When a vendor increases a price beyond a price point (say to a price slightly above price point B), sales volume decreases by an amount more than proportional to the price increase. This decrease in quantity-demanded more than offsets the additional revenue from the increased unit-price. As a result, total revenue (price multiplied by quantity-demanded) decreases when a firm raises its price beyond a price point. Technically, the price elasticity of demand is low (inelastic) at a price lower than the price point (steep section of the demand curve), and high (elastic) at a price higher than a price point (gently sloping part of the demand curve). Firms commonly set prices at existing price-points as a marketing strategy.[citation needed]

Three main reasons exist to have price points:

Imagine, I have this [13]*price point* of my wigs, needing to be purchase at my whole sale price at $2,000. Less is always better, but more or a higher price, there is almost no profit available.

You see, when my wholesale company has gone, to let's say China, or Bangladesh, to convene and to commence a greater business transaction for them, but the price point that they had come to was $2,100, instead of $2,000...

There are two probabilities at this point, with this new data and newer price point...

The first, for certainly, is that I probably would lose my composure.

You see, this wholesaler, lost me as a customer..

By now, my loyal and allegiant clients, or my ardently devoted customers, expect and foreknow and presumably conjecture, my normal and regulated price point, to a Tee.

Now, with this new strategically terrible for my business, *price point*, I would have had to execute a higher price and therefore, precariously advertize this newer higher change format.

I had then the potential to lose and suffer the greater loss, of approximately 20% of my clients.

If, I would have a major change in the price, whether it would be a reduction, or an elevated price, I still would lose even more customers, at an astounding percentage of 40%. Meaning, that approximately 40% of my customers would not shop by me. Now, if I increased my price by 30%, approximately 40% of my customers would lose confidence in me..

You see, even in the appositions of pricing...

In businesses, even loyal customers, will leave your customer base at a minimal 20% decrease, thinking that something is amiss..

You see, these greater consumers might imply, or come to the conclusions, that they are not receiving the qualities that they were receiving in the past parts, of you selling the exact wig structure, or similar, at an even slightly higher price.

This is a greater Thesis, on this subject matter than you can even understand..

Proof of the pudding was, that I kept on having to answer questions about the hair qualities and the cap constructions, when I went on sale.

Please realize that, when I was at a higher price point, this never happened, my customers just assumed that I was selling the better qualities and that they were receiving their monies worth, which was the realities.

Please realize that, the price point for my customers, the average price that they would have had to pay to purchase my wigs, was in this very case was $3,600. If I had to elevate, or charge more for the same product, and let's say charge $4,000, potentially and in the probables and in the for certainties, I would lose most of my clientele.

You see, even if I changed the product, or my inventory, to a micro niche product..

The possibilities, that I would have lost 60% of my customer base, was imminent, if I brought in a product that this exact customer base, truly did not want, or like.

Please, never "switch and bait".

Please realize, like I already mentioned, if the product was an upgrade and in the exact "energetically greater particles" of what my customers would have wished for, as we talked about. The opposing forces of losing clients would happen.

You see, I would then, truly jump start my business again and the profits would be greater than anyone could ever imagine.

This whole exercise, is one of the scarier and trying parts of doing business. Change can be a "hit or miss", in general.

So, the moral of this teachings is, that we are needing to keep the integrity of our product, if we are doing well.

Adding additional upgrades, are vital to the lastabities and the longevity of our clients and therefore, profitabilities.

Please realize that, we are needing to constantly up-grade and improve our "product or service", slightly or in a grandeur performa gratis, ways, of giving our customers "more than they bargained for" or more value for their money.

You see, up-grades and improvements in our "product" are mandatory and must be implemented, in order to facilitate and "keep the money rolling in" or have a greater cash flow and create an infrastructure, of our successes in the opportune ways, of truly being a successful and solidifyably, quality Flagship structure.

Next on the agenda, of the creations of that one greater store, that are also in the mandatory parts of "must does", is to **purchase every single web site** with our Title, or banner, or name, or partial name in it and in the main parts of the genre in it, even if you only use one now.

- Even, the Websites must be purchased and possessed and literally seized right away, with the conception of your name.

I truly mean right away. Each name that is similar, or analogous, or complementary, or homogeneous, or in any way related is also important to purchase and apprehend at this point in time.

- I also "demand and command", that you **retrieve every phone number**, in the genre of your business, or store, immediately!!

You must acquire and obtain every phone number, that is associated with your name, as well as, for any phone numbers that are in the acronym of your name, of your store, or business, meaning the first initial of your name and therefore, be ready for the growth of your business where the needs for more appropriate web sights and more pages, or more storage, or ample mega bites are retrievable in the nearer, or father futuristically greater and more successful time periods.

- This is a must. Most companies are lax about this requirement, but they have spent many mega bucks, where I intend to inhabit some beach, enjoying life, in it's stead.

You must have a pictorial logo, that is exactly like your companies name, in the form of easily conjoining the conceptual parts of the logo and your company's name and a pictorial attachment and supplement, or ornament is vital!!

Yes, Coca Cola never had one and therefore they spend so far the astronomically capital of over a trillion dollars in advertisements.

Chapter Five

Review

1. Please, iterate on a few more must haves, that a Flagship must consist of?

_____

_____

_____

_____

_____

_____

_____

_____

_____

_____

_____

_____

_____

_____

_____

_____

_____

_____

_____

_____

_____

_____

_____

_____

_____

_____

2. Please, describe what it truly means to "think big" in the aspect of creating
   1. Flagship Quality stores

   _____
   _____
   _____
   _____
   _____
   _____
   _____
   _____
   _____
   _____
   _____
   _____
   _____

   2. businesses

   _____
   _____
   _____
   _____
   _____
   _____
   _____
   _____
   _____
   _____
   _____
   _____

3. any other reciprocally greater formats of earning monies?

_____

_____

_____

_____

_____

_____

_____

_____

_____

_____

_____

_____

3. Please, elucidate in what ways a Flagship Quality formats, of any venue must be systematically inclined and described each itemized particle?

_____

_____

_____

_____

_____

_____

_____

_____

_____

_____

_____

_____

4. Please, imagine that you are hiring and in the process of the interviewing of prospective employees, for your upcoming store, that you have added the extra monetary and other parts of assuring that your store is of a quality Flagship styling. What would you look for in your employees and what calibration are you looking to hire, or to have found in your personnel that you will be hiring. Pretend, that you are interviewing them right now?

_____

_____

_____

_____

_____

_____

_____

_____

_____

_____

_____

_____

_____

_____

_____

_____

_____

_____

_____

_____

_____

_____

5. Please, understandably iterate how lowering your prices, can destroy your business and chase away your already loyal clients.. please, remember that it cost approximately $500 to acquire each new consumer through revenues of advertising and other Branding parts?

_____

_____

_____

_____

_____

_____

_____

_____

_____

_____

6. Please, in similarities for raising prices, conduct the same standardized applicational elucidate on how it can also destroy your already Branded store, or business?

_____

_____

_____

_____

_____

_____

_____

_____

_____

7. Please, tell me what the biggest blunder of purchasing merchandise from abroad, meaning China, or Italy, or France, or England, or India and many more places, is?

_____

_____

_____

_____

_____

_____

_____

_____

_____

_____

8. Please, describe the differences between a regular store and a Flagship Quality store and if I am creating a business, or opening up a store, should I only consider making it a Flagship Quality store, or business and why?

_____

_____

_____

_____

_____

_____

_____

_____

_____

_____

_____

_____

_____

_____

_____

_____

_____

9. In the analogy of a cubby and each drawer is ultimately organized, please, analytically masterfully get this right. Always take the higher road to stardom and thereby, please articulate and perceivably orchestrate the itemized list, of why I should commence a greater Flagship quality anything, so as to never cut down, on organization and customer satisfaction?

10. _____

_____

_____

_____

_____

_____

_____

_____

_____

_____

_____

_____

_____

_____

_____

_____

Chapter Six

The art of "Piggybacking"

You see, at this point in time, it is so fundamentality vital that I explain and instruct and disclose and reveal and of course unravel to you all, that there is such a thing in business, that mimics the action of **"Piggybacking"** and in this chapter, I will explain to you a few aspects of conjuring these images, to our businesses benefits and therefore, being able to utilize these tools, to advance every part of our "Branding" and "Flagship" venture.

Please realize that, It is vital to our analyzations that you all truly learn the art of "Piggybacking".

First of all, what is the truer meaning of "Piggybacking" when it comes to a business start ups, or a retail grandeur opening?

You see, when we open up a business, or a retail location, our biggest hurdle is getting the right exact customers, or clients, or patrons, that will buy our merchandise or utilize our service, like a Doctor or a Dentist or a manicurist or even a hair dresser..

We require loyalty in greater amounts in order to constantly have the flow of business that is required in order to truly be successful..

We must procure and we are in dire need of and for sure, require recurring customers.. return clientele and "regulars"..

You see, the normal process of this happenings, is to have a greater following and thereby, a successful store, or businesses can in a good corporation, or a well established business, or business in a better situation can require approximately a good ten years, if we are lucky, to be a success story..

Please realize that, the problem is that in the meantime the possibilities of us going out of business are much greater, if we have carry costs and losses for not having the "turnover" of our inventory, that is vitally necessary for a greater successful business..

So, one of the techniques that is cost effective and thereby, a better usage of our "start up" capital, is the venue of leasing a store, or a space, that has the abilities of ensuing the "Piggyback" techniques, of succeeding in a much faster venue that the norm and thereby, being an "Overnight Success"!!

You see, there is such a thing as an energetic makeup, of every parts of our lives...
... of even successes and achievements in our business and ascendancy and advancement in every parts of our lives..

You see again.. the energetical make up of successes in the venues of business, of the utilizations of a "Piggyback", is much more accelerated and stronger velocities and faster build ups of your business and so much "safer" in the ways of the "surer" parts of successes..

Let me explain..

Please realize that, the energetic make up of a business, or any venture, requires a minimum of ten years, to be an actual overnight success.. from the time of conception to the time of the tangible and verifiable capital successes..

Let me iterate and elucidate and explain in a preferred metaphor and homology of a Tsunami and a surfer..

Imagine, that there is a greater tsunami and in a very augmented structural parts, of the wind waves and swells being in a format of a stochastic process, or the generation of greater height and flow velocities, or strength..

You see, the Tsunami is an energetically greater structure, that takes about ten years to construct, or generate, just like the metaphorically greater mass parts of a business structure, or any venture framework, or apparatus..

From the time of that first butterfly flapping its wings, like in the "[14]Butterfly Effect" theory, where if the butterfly just

---

[14]   The butterfly effect is the concept that small causes can have large effects. Initially, it was used with weather prediction but later the term became a metaphor used in and out of science.[1]

In chaos theory, the butterfly effect is the sensitive dependence on initial conditions in which a small change in one state of a deterministic nonlinear system can result in large differences in a later state.[2] The name, coined by Edward Lorenz for the effect which had been known long before, is derived from the metaphorical example of the details of a hurricane (exact time of formation, exact path taken) being influenced by minor perturbations such as the flapping of the wings of a distant butterfly several weeks earlier. Lorenz discovered the effect when he observed that runs of his weather model with initial condition data that was rounded in a seemingly inconsequential flaps its wings in China, the ripple effect years later, is a possible greater storm, or even a tsunami..

You see, if there is any formats of [15]obstructions to the ocean, even in the further parts of any country, or island,

---

manner would fail to reproduce the results of runs with the unrounded initial condition data. A very small change in initial conditions had created a significantly different outcome.[3]

The idea that small causes may have large effects in general and in weather specifically was used from Henri Poincaré to Norbert Wiener. Edward Lorenz's work placed the concept of instability of the atmosphere onto a quantitative base and linked the concept of instability to the properties of large classes of dynamic systems which are undergoing nonlinear dynamics and deterministic chaos. [1][clarification needed]

The butterfly effect is exhibited by very simple systems. For example, the randomness of the outcomes of throwing dice depends on this characteristic to amplify small differences in initial conditions—the precise direction, thrust, and orientation of the throw—into significantly different dice paths and outcomes, which makes it virtually impossible to throw dice exactly the same way twice.

[15] The Butterfly Effect: This effect grants the power to cause a hurricane in China to a butterfly flapping its wings in New Mexico. It may take a very long time, but the connection is real. If the butterfly had not flapped its wings at just the right point in space/time, the hurricane would not have happened. A more rigorous way to express this is that small changes in the initial conditions lead to drastic changes in the results. Our lives are an ongoing demonstration of this principle. Who knows what the long-term effects of teaching millions of kids about chaos and fractals will be?
Unpredictability: Because we can never know all the initial conditions of a complex system in sufficient (i.e. perfect) detail, we cannot hope to predict the ultimate fate of a complex system. Even slight errors in measuring the state of a system will be amplified dramatically, rendering any prediction useless. Since it is impossible to measure the effects of all the butterflies (etc) in the World, accurate long-range weather prediction will always remain impossible.

or even Iceland, or a mountain that had an avalanche, or even just water skiers, or snow skiers and it effected the same united ocean, even in the minutest ways..

Ugh!!

You just started a Tsunami..

Imagine then that a tsunami, or a storm formats, are therefore, starting the energetic pathways in that very same ocean but, most probably across the world and on the other side of your existence..

Order / Disorder Chaos is not simply disorder. Chaos explores the transitions between order and disorder, which often occur in surprising ways.

Mixing: Turbulence ensures that two adjacent points in a complex system will eventually end up in very different positions after some time has elapsed. Examples: Two neighboring water molecules may end up in different parts of the ocean or even in different oceans. A group of helium balloons that launch together will eventually land in drastically different places. Mixing is thorough because turbulence occurs at all scales. It is also nonlinear: fluids cannot be unmixed.

Feedback: Systems often become chaotic when there is feedback present. A good example is the behavior of the stock market. As the value of a stock rises or falls, people are inclined to buy or sell that stock. This in turn further affects the price of the stock, causing it to rise or fall chaotically.

Fractals: A fractal is a never-ending pattern. Fractals are infinitely complex patterns that are self-similar across different scales. They are created by repeating a simple process over and over in an ongoing feedback loop. Driven by recursion, fractals are images of dynamic systems – the pictures of Chaos. Geometrically, they exist in between our familiar dimensions. Fractal patterns are extremely familiar, since nature is full of fractals. For instance: trees, rivers, coastlines, mountains, clouds, seashells, hurricanes, etc.

But, this energetically masterfully complicated yet predictable energy, will only be totally realized in a greater strength, in about ten years of "picking up speed" and being altered like that metaphorically greater analogy of a snowball on top of a mountain, that became larger and larger, as it hits the bottom of the mountain.

Imagine, then that you have a man, or a woman that surfs and they ride the metaphorically scarier tsunami wave..

That is what truer "piggybacking" is about..
The ability to ride a wave, that has been altered and has been "in the works", so to speak, for about ten years and counting, otherwise the surfer would just be riding the normal everyday waves.

So..
If you are starting out, you will acquiescence and accept and ratify and acknowledge, that any venture necessitate and desiderates, at least ten years to develop and grow that very business into a "golden egg" or a "cash cow", so to speak..

Let us start, at the very beginning of this conceptual particles, of understanding the energetically greater parts, of the why's of this happening, in the realer ways of a start up business..

First of all, please remember that the business that you are "piggybacking" with, most probably has been in business for at least ten years, if they are truly successful..

...and therefore, if you "connect", or conjointly and network with and associate your own venue to that store, or business, by opening up a booth, or leasing next door to them, or nearby, or in the same complex of the exact mall, or in a medical center, or a Doctor, or Lawyers facilities..

You see, there traffic will be your traffic and their clientele will be your patronage and their correlation to the public and their advertisements and their structures and sales and their gains will effect you, as well..

Please realize that, in such a greater senecio, you will not have the hold-up, or the impediment, or the remission of the "wait time", which is truly the norm and the expected creation time gestation and thereby, the requirement time period of developments of your structural ideas, and necessitates the period of those ten years, to be that "success story", so to speak.

You must, please then realize, that the store that you are "piggybacking" with, has already "done their time". They have have already nurtured and developed and allocated and severely augmented their business, to meld with their clients.. after ten years and counting..not to forget, the energy was surging and growing..

.. and spent on advertising..

So, that very 10 year time period of developing his clientele, is a "done deal" and therefore, notwithstanding, you are an accompaniment of another business, or a different venue of receiving's of something of value and therefore, the success rate and the achievements, are at a much faster and ameliorated and preeminent and prodigious pace.

We need to automatically learn and apprentice and be trained to "Piggy Back" and learn techniques on every juncture, that we can and procure as many different formats, of this same energetic formation/shortcut to success, being that the 10 years of being an overnight success has been attained, and in the similar venues of receiving's of the same end products.. unsurpassed and a grandeur venue of successes.

You see, I will be doing exactly that, in this chapter. I, will be enlightening and instructing you, in the simplest formats for the assurance of your truer successes, and in the more natural parts of the creation processes, or developing your business structures, with the metaphorical egg already inside of your chicken, so to speak, even concerning having the egg be constantly nurtured, even by others in the "Piggy Back" ways of nurturing, after its birthing.

I hope to achieve the parts, where I will explain to you, how to take the birthed egg, or the future parts of your very greater business, or the venue of producing anything for monetary reasons, or for any reasons, already securely implanted in the infrastructure and "Piggy Back" in a secure and structured ways, of why did I not think of doing that. In the most natural and uncomplicated venues of successes!!

One of the techniques, that we will be incorporating in our Piggy Back tutorial, is utilized in the Early Child Program.

The Technique used by children are being taught to read through "Sight Words". They are shown a pictorial and thereby, they memorize the spelling and the entireties of the picture.

As a Branding parts of our Program, every single time that we mention our name, ANYWHERE, you will be adding your verbal logos, as well as your pictorial insignia, AUTOMATICALLY, that already have been marketed, as I will be explaining shortly..

The pictorial logo, has to have the qualities and attributes and **conditioning** of immediately, just by instantaneously showing the population a picture..

We thereby, will be able to cognize your enterprise and recognize your very esteemed establishment and distinguish your very syndicate or business..

We will then actualize, what forum or apparatus that we are talking about right away, and what our venue of sales are, without delay, in a split second..

Just like and in similarity to the Early Child "Sight Words" and in congruence and in homogeneity and in likeness, of a different established and preeminent and celebrious and of course, a well know company, that sashays in the public eyes and is already well established.

Please, remember that we are talking about "Piggybacking" in this parts and thereby, the sight word could be a pun on an already established name brand, or just a similar avenue of the pictorial logo parts, of already being well known and famous.

You see, in order for this to truly work, we are needed to also incorporate what we have learned about, utilizing our product in our name, as well..

Another aspect, that must be met is that the sight words and the emblem, must incorporate or contain a harmonious insignia, that tell us, the future customers, what you are selling and the quality that we should be expected, or modulated at every corner of this store, in the important homogeneous particles of being a predictable store, or business, in the positive.

You see, the most strenuous parts and the impenetrably and troublesome and formidable and for sure problematic and the most expensive parts in any business, is to truly get your clients and lining up and constantly increasing and aggrandize your customer base AND THE RETURN FACTORS OF LOYAL CUSTOMERS.

How we can we endear and gravitate and attract and captivate our clients, or customers without the higher expense and investment and of course outlay.. and there went our profits?

In order to commit one client to our store, it cost us in advertisements as least $500 per.

Thereby... we are needing to "Piggyback", an please make sure that you are incorporating an established or well advertised company that has existed for at least ten years or that tHey are also piggy baking on a different greater company that has also existed for about ten years and counting.

Get ready for another aspect of "Piggybacking"..

Please realize that, this is the best by far,"Piggy Back" technique...

You see, if we lease a store, or showroom, that is in a totally different venue and personification, as well as for diverse inventory and therefore, your inventory, or store, or service, will accentuate your neighboring store's wares....

Imagine, working in tandem.

Please realize that, your neighbors have been there for much longer than you and that, they have been cultivating customers and most probably, they have already laid out the expenditures of the $500 per.

They have what you are needing, clients and customers and the stability of a recurring business.

You do not!!

So, the trick of this "Piggy Back", is to make sure that the neighboring stores, or showrooms are not only successful and prosperous and profitable, but have the clients that would love your micro-niche, as well.

You must compliment and you must work in alliance and harmony together. Never be each other competitions, or rivals. You both will "Piggy Back" eventually, off each other and thereby, be such greater asset to each other.

You see, eventually your niche will only complements your neighbors store, or showroom and therefore, eventually you will reciprocate and attract customers, or clients to their store, or Showroom as well.

You will both work in tandem for each success, as well as for the both of your united successes.

You see, "Piggy Backing" is strategically a better way to jump start and inaugurate and initiate a business, without the expenditures and the never ending advertising, but....

I have this epic, of a truer episode that ensued and befell me, a few years back...

Now, please realize that, I was about to sign and acquiesce on a lease agreement for a store location, that was right next door to a considerably populous discount supermarket, that received and sold merchandise to at least 1,000 women customers a day and my luck we shared the same stereo type of archetype and representation personality type and "Avatar" and archetype cast, that would be my potentially, hopefully nearer futuristic prospect patrons..

Imagine, how fast and how easily and accelerated, that I could have build up and superstruct my business..

Imagine then..
..just by being next door, how many clients would be curious, as to what my store was about,if they already not only had a parking space, which this greater store format had, but also just had the convenience of being in a location, where most of their daily and routine shopping needs were met..

I acknowledged and deduced, that even if I just put my businesses logo, or my very small shingle on this location, without ever creating the retail space, that I hoped to assemble and initiate and inaugurate, this location, that is right next door to this megastore, would be of the greater in the economical "bargain basement" budgeted advertising in the optimum and unsurpassed and best evaluations venues, that is possible...

..plus the "Piggybacking" was a perfect aspect of even more economic and financial savings..
.. which adds up, to more profits in my pocket.

So..

I felt like I won the lottery ticket of locations, at bargain basement prices of rents and the austere parts of never suffering again, from being a navigator of just "chasing my tail", just like most of us do in any business format..

Ok..

So, I was already in the process with my lease monies, in a check format.

You see, I already went to the owner prior to his inaugurating and him hiring Realestate Agents.

Ugh!!
I truly tried to give that fated check straight to the owner, to solidify and fortify the deal..

He then told me, that there was one person prior aforementioned, that gave him a deposit on this property, as well..

As you can conceivably envisage and imagine..

Ugh!!

I was in the formats of, "I lost a deal of a life time"!!

Imagine, then a week later..
You will not believe my luck!

You must realize that, the owner of this retail location emailed me, that it would be possible to actualize my dream, of opening up a Flagship Retail location, at his site and thereby..

I was up and in for the chance at leasing this store formation, but I needed to move swiftly and in precision..

..and with his evacuated personality of being a control freak and therefore, I was like..

Ugh!!
`

Just, say yes already..

You see, I had a partner and he was in this deal with me and he reneged on this Flagship store, that I was in the formats of launching and initiating and because of that, I did not undergo and go through with, in my opinion, greater retail space.

Every time that I passed by this very store, I was in the "should have, could have, and would have", formats of wishing that I would have closed that deal..

Please realize that, over two years later, I happened to pass by the other day and I could not believe what I was seeing...

That greater retail store, that I was going to be using to piggy back off, closed its doors and went belly up.

So...
Get ready for this added lesson...
Never get a retail location, or piggy back off any retail, or wholesale location, or any format of business locations whatsoever, unless...

..you have introduced yourself and thereby, talked to the owners, or other Doctors, or Dentists, or beauticians, or any formats of neighbors and asked them, how they were doing and to tell you more about his retail location and his patrons.

..and now, a few other possibilities...

Perhaps, you are wanting to join a medical building, or a beauticians dream of being in a spa location, or to have a small booth in a Bergdorf Goodman, or in a Saks Fifth Ave, or a different upscale store.

Perchance, you are dreaming of being in a upscale mall, or shopping center..

These are all greater ways of "Piggy Backing"...

Please realize that, even if a store seams busy, it does not mean that they are actually busy with sales. Getting to know the "next door" neighboring owners and conversing with them and inquiring them and grilling them with as many questions as possible, will help you to decide the better outcome, of wether you are making the right choice in your "Piggy Back" locations, which of course, I highly recommend going in that venue of starting a newer business.

Please remember that, you will be also, eventually going to help and add value to this neighbor as well, with bringing in more clients through your own forms of advertisements, or becoming more of a shopping area, that is more worthwhile for a patron to find a parking space for.. these clients will be shared, eventually as well.

You see, on a few occasions, I attended a business lecture and discourse in my community and someone coached and educated and taught me, in the ways of truly individualizing and thereby, masterly in the truer ways of comprehending and the better ways of understanding. That precise microsecond, where everything comes together and you understand clearly, what was taught to you and how to transform it into wisdom.

One of the lecturers articulated and recounted said something noteworthy and in my worthy of inaugurating an in the greater applications of us, finding a location for our greater "Flagships". "He said, be a "Secret Agent" and investigate and administer appraisals and verify your new location, that you are about to lease, or purchase and preview and asses that areas walking traffic and verify the population, or inspect the car traffic.

Scout out and assess, how many persons and possibilities of patrons, would per haps be your customers, or clients.

Thereby...Minus 90% of your findings.. and that is your truer potential client base.

I sat and ensconced myself, the entirety of a day, in my car and scouted the areas..

I payed special attention to their wigs and consideration to and special scrutiny of their types of hairdos and due diligence of the amount and type of shopping bags, with their very purchases of the day..

I should have also observed and with regard duly noted and analyzed and guesstimated, to descry and be apprised of, if these very neighbors patrons were just "window shoppers" and therefore, had no bags, or purchases.. but I just thought of that now!!

I apprehended and gathered much important relevant predictions and prognostications..

I surmised that the evaluations and the forth bearers and the calculations were in the positive for all of these evaluations, if I were going to pick this formats of commencing of this very expedited and expeditively faster ways of being an overnight success...

You see, the most important and vital and exigent parts, of opening up a business is the cash flow..

Some of our considerations and doubts are in the question forums of...

Will I have patrons purchasing and creating the flow of business?

...whether with walking traffic, or driving traffic, I would truly be able to be successful, in the ways of the "piggybacking" style, of a quickly enhanced success.

Why did I think that I would have won the lottery tickets of being in a Flagship quality store?

You see, because I was "Piggy Backing" off another two greater mega-stores.

We need to understand that, in this business you will be needing to make a calculation, or a judgement call, or an inspectors assessments on how many persons, that are conceivably possibly and potentially going to want to purchase something in your stores and thereby, be return customers..

These forecasts and appraisals and computations and guesstimations are determined by a few factors..

The formats, that I have presented to you at the end of this chapter, will be of a greater consideration and a component in masterly alleviating this calculations, to achieve the better particle of understand that evaluations, as well as, a few other factors, that I will review from other chapters of this book, that we have spoken about already..

You see, the chapter on "Piggybacking" is also, a greater component of revenues, as well as for a greater customer base, that will support the avenue of your unobstructed and commodities in the fashionistá ways of creating a well running business, or client based Flagship quality store, or service oriented commodity.

Please, be realistic and then minus 90%. There is your true potential measure and aggregation and irrevocably promising future loyal customers.

Chapter Six

Review

1. Please, annotate and demonstrate, what a truer legal good energetically piggy backing, truly means and please, give me an example?

_____

_____

_____

_____

_____

_____

_____

_____

_____

_____

_____

_____

_____

_____

_____

_____

_____

_____

_____

_____

_____

_____

_____

_____

_____

2. Please, decode and name, as many ways that you can muster, on how you can truly piggy back, in any business structure.
   1. The formats and convocation of a wholesale business structure forum?

_____

_____

_____

_____

_____

_____

_____

_____

_____

_____

_____

_____

_____

_____

_____

_____

_____

_____

_____

_____

_____

_____

_____

2. In the apparatus and formats, of a greater Flagship Store?

_____

_____

_____

_____

_____

_____

_____

_____

_____

_____

_____

_____

_____

_____

_____

_____

_____

_____

_____

_____

_____

_____

_____

_____

_____

_____

_____

_____

_____

3. In the conclave and formats of a E-Commerce.

_____
_____
_____
_____
_____
_____
_____
_____
_____
_____
_____
_____
_____
_____
_____
_____
_____
_____
_____
_____
_____
_____
_____
_____
_____
_____
_____
_____

4. In the Avenue and formats of a service oriented businesses, not unlike a Practitioner, or a lawyers practice.

_____

_____

_____

_____

_____

_____

_____

_____

_____

_____

_____

_____

_____

_____

_____

_____

_____

_____

_____

_____

_____

_____

_____

_____

_____

3. Please, reintegrate and exemplify, why piggy backing is vital to the success of any newbie business?

_____

_____

_____

_____

_____

_____

_____

_____

_____

_____

_____

_____

_____

_____

_____

_____

_____

_____

_____

_____

_____

_____

_____

_____

4. In the formats and configurations of a masterful Energetical wave length of piggy backing, how does this phenomenon truly work in our favor, in the business world?

_____

_____

_____

_____

_____

_____

_____

_____

_____

_____

_____

_____

_____

_____

_____

_____

_____

_____

_____

_____

_____

_____

_____

_____

5. How are childhood "sight words" in simailarities to the Branding venues and improvisations of our companies and how could we best masterly achieve the uttermost and the foreseeable multifarious results?

_____

_____

_____

_____

_____

_____

_____

_____

_____

_____

_____

_____

_____

_____

_____

_____

_____

_____

_____

_____

_____

_____

_____

_____

Chapter Seven

Knowing your patrons

Imagine, that for every client it necessitates approximately $500, to embrace them into being your loyal customer, if you are lucky..

You see, the most basic and and requisite and significant and vital to any truly successful and moneymaking business, and the most considerably and foremost and essential importune ingredient and module, that you can pray and crave for and truly hope for in any business environment, **is to truly be cognizant and understand you clients, in every aspect of their shopping and materialistic needs.**

If you truly understand and truly individualize these clients, your cash flow and hopefully, many friendships will naturally blossom and flourish.

By undoubtedly knowing and cognizant and discern your clients taste and their druthers, of their spending outlay proneness and penchants, when it come to to their very greater purchasing and shopping ways..

Imagine, that you can truly pinpoint what their desideratum and further requirements and needs are, with certainly, certitude, credence, with so many fewer inaccuracies and miscalculations and mistakes and so many fewer **"sale racks" = losses.**

Without a doubt when we are a stereotype, or a cliché, or a typecast, or a standardization, or a "Stepford", or "Avatar", we have the abilities and the aptitude and capacity to easily understand our clients, better personalities and easily understand their commercial and purchasing requisites needs.

Imagine, truly knowing what are their favorite colors, or preferred attire vestments, or garment types, or styling? Are their any culturally important aspects to their garment purchases, or any religious specifications to their attire..

..maybe a school uniform, that has to be even to a greater specifications...

We must know their mentality and the mindset and quotient of every customer, in the stereo type groups, or just perhaps, just in the fashionistá venues of only yearning for and necessitating and hankering for the higher fashions, of the "trends"..

Please realize that, the only way that I could ever truly explain and elucidate and firmly demonstrate to you, that the most determining factor and paramount factor, besides the quality of the niche item's, that you are selling and of course the price budget, is **understanding your clients and thereby return customers..**

..and thereby, making fewer mistakes that cost us and are detrimental and devastating to our NET profits..

Please, realize that these inaccuracies are just the worst particles of having a retail location, or a wholesale business, or any inventory based business..

Please, elucidate and individualize that if you have clothing, or merchandise on the sale rack, there went your profits sitting in the back of the store, mis-happened and misshaped and most probably, a greater amassed wear and tear and chances are, that they are also, soiled.

So, here goes appreciation and gratitude and recognition and indebtedness, of each and every customer. Without each one, without exception, we have no business.

We must treat and gratify each customer, as if they are our only solitary patrons.. like they are the most importunate and esteemed clients.. even if they hardly and comparatively infrequently, purchase anything.

Please, remember that always!!

Clients are our commodity. They are our business. They are our cash flow and our wealth..

Now, there is also the possibility and plausibility and prospect of bringing in clients, through Social Net Working and through your Web sites. That is a whole other venue of bringing in our greatest commodity, our greater assets, our customers.

Please realize that, every client, or customer in particular is unequalled in every way, and that I could have ever truly understood and inferred and accepted and appreciated, in the most positive ways..

Understanding our commodity, our clients;

An example; More to presume and understand, for instance if my store sells women's clothing, in the range of fifty to sixty year old evaluation of the trends of our seasonally greater time periods. Conservative type clothing, for let's say older woman that are Church going type or the old fashioned in the ways of modesty, or just a perfectly matched ensemble.

Maybe, I will add.. these same patrons.. enjoy the added accessories of wearing a hat and a sweater.

You see, I just honed in on getting this group of women to want to purchase, from my selection and my viewpoint on the fashionistá avenues for their stereo type..

These same greater patrons, will enjoy my taste fused with their gratified yearnings in "my store"..

You see, the reason being is that, because I made it my specialty and my métier and my livelihood, and my essence of my business to understand and discern my clients, in order to sincerely market what their very greater not only yearnings, but my store became their absentee personal shopper as well as a place where they feel loved and esteemed and appreciated.

You see again...now I became their "personal Shopper" and effortless and commodious and easier place to shop.

Now, I understand their body shapes and their desires and needs and therefore, my clothing will be an advantageous and comfortable and better fit in them.

You see, now they will not only enjoy and and receive greater pleasure and love to shop by my location.

If we act like a personal shopper, and respectful and nurturing, thereby, when they come in the store, they will yearn and relish for your taste and the majority and the preponderance and superior parts, of what they are viewing, is exactly their taste and love.

These very same patrons, will not have to hunt through every garment to find the one piece, that they love, the one piece that is close to their resembling ways, of their aptitude for styling.. everything, every particle of my inventory, is in that ways of being perfect for them..

If they are in the busier parts... less time wasted!!

Less for the hated "bottomless pit" of the sale rack..more deficit..

So, be specific...

In the "target practice"..

Know whom your client is, or your "Avatar", or whom is your beneficiallies are, when it comes to purchasing your wares, or your inventory and thereby your doors will be staying open at that very point in that time period when you have enough loyal patrons to vacate your greater fashionistá habiliments.

Appreciation!!

So..

I have compiled a simpler format.. not the greatest, a bit amateurishly written...but, necessary or I would have left it out..

There are sites, that publish more professionally written formats, but, the questions that I have written, are of the ones, that I thought were more necessary to the truer and the delving of the better consideration of our beneficiaries, our clients, or our customers and our greater assets.

But, for most of you this will be sufficient and please, add as many questions as you can.

By the way, there are many surveys that seem to have much better formats, but, I truly individualize, that my amateurish survey will help you in a better ways, of purchasing the better inventories and in the end results, the financially better for you formats..

Here is a preview, on many of the important questions, that will help you create a better understanding and facilitate, such a better business increment.

.. and guess what?

Less in the hated sales rack.

I have gifted you, at the parts of this book of the index, a format that you can procure and evaluate and print out and give to your patrons.

Please, administer to your very important clients, compensation for filling this out. A gift certificate? A 🎁.

This information is so vital to the successes of your store and thereby, you can even have a study at the beginning of each season, to view the new line, and give these special customers the first opportunity, like a trunk show, or a fashion show, before you put the order in.

You can thereby, procure information that they would appreciate, by asking them if they would obviously purchase, or demonstrate a greater ways of loving what you are purchasing for the next segments of your seasonal attire...

..or, perhaps.. ..if they would highly recomend their evaluation to others like themselves if asked..

.. or, if they were to structure a program their very home to sell these garments as well..

You see, if you have a consumer that is a greater personality, or a sales person personality, please realize that you are doubly blessed..

Let each guest be cognizant, that they were the chosen ones and that each patron's requisite, to fill out the formats of whether they would purchase these evaluations of these garments, or if they enjoy the styling, or if they would recomend to their friend any of the garments, that are in the trunk show, or in the fashion show..

please have fun with this very greater idea..

Serve Hors d'oeuvre, or playful cookies, in the formats of garments...

Turn this evening, or day affair into a game formats..

Project Runway here we come!! In our own show room, or in our store, or in a better parts of the theaters, or in Bryant Park.

The vital importance, is to make certain that you truly understood and was informed about the right personality, that is the main "type" or "Avatar" of the quality, or classification and genus purchaser and patron for your store.

Please realize that, **understanding the mentalities and the dress habits and proclivities and in general the state of their better parts of their spending habits and consuetude ways of their buying practices of this group, or any category, is vital to you success.**

If one has issues understanding the mentality of any group that is part of your store, or business, please hire a few people from that particular group..

Let them educate you in their very greater and most probably complicated culture.

Please, then give them a coupon to use right away, or offer a discount in you store for interviewing them.

You see, this scenario is a common one..

Imagine, that you have this modernized organized beautiful store and you purchased for this very season the mostly gorgeous pant suits. You are in love with every single suit and cannot believe what a greater deal that you have made..

Ugh!!

Guess what?

Your clients only wear dresses, with a matching sweater..

With this information coming too late, you can have a terrible season, with a greater loss and now I would say, the possibility of bankruptcy is close.

Sales rack?

We must know and understand your client's buying and purchasing habits and fashionable parts of them. It is important to understand your clients needs to us, in the portionate particles that is pertaining, to our elite parts of our development of our stores, or business, in the greatest parts of the most important parts...

Customer Satisfaction!!

Please, always be kind and generous without losing profits and always think in the clients ways of, "what would I want, if I were my patron".

Please realize that, this is amateurish, but a much funnier ways of getting the information, that we are needing to acquire, to better our reciprocalities and create a greater return customer care, as well as, for us to be very profitable, with fewer minor "mistakes", or losses..

Midterm

1. Please, reiterate how does truly discerning and thereby, understanding your patrons, effect your business and denouement and therefore, effectuate and progenerate and stimulate your cash flow?

_____

_____

_____

_____

_____

_____

_____

_____

_____

_____

_____

_____

_____

_____

_____

_____

_____

_____

_____

_____

_____

2. Please, disclose and expound on an example, of how you can lose your shirt, so to speak, in business, if you do not truly cognize and truly care enough and put heart into your business, to understand your Avatar?

_____

_____

_____

_____

_____

_____

_____

_____

_____

_____

_____

_____

_____

_____

_____

_____

_____

_____

_____

_____

_____

_____

_____

3. Please, actualize and author a store, or a wholesale company, or an E-Commerce business, or self employed service oriented business structure.. then please answer and clarify and address these questions.
   1. Whom is your authentic Avatar, please chronicle and portray a picture and an image and describe every detail possible.

   _____
   _____
   _____
   _____
   _____
   _____
   _____
   _____
   _____
   _____
   _____
   _____
   _____
   _____
   _____
   _____
   _____
   _____
   _____
   _____
   _____
   _____
   _____

2. Please, disclose to me, do they wear name Brands?

_____

_____

_____

_____

_____

3. Please, publish where do they shop?

_____

_____

_____

_____

_____

4. Please, communicate which restaurants do they eat at and at what average cost per?

_____

_____

_____

_____

_____

_____

5. Please, impart to me, which community center are they affiliated with?

_____

_____

_____

_____

_____

6. Please, expose to me, which synagogue they are affiliated with?

_____

_____

_____

_____

_____

_____

_____

7. Please, disclose to me which Church, if any, they are affiliated with?

_____

_____

_____

_____

_____

_____

_____

8. Please, promulgate to me where their children, if this applicable, attend school?

_____

_____

_____

_____

_____

_____

_____

9. Please, release to me how many children on average do they rear?

_____
_____
_____
_____
_____
_____
_____
_____
_____

10. Please, divulge to me what kind of homes do they live in?

_____
_____
_____
_____
_____
_____

11. Please, evince to me where they vacation and how frequent in an annum times period and what types of vacations, they are interested in?

_____
_____
_____
_____
_____
_____

12. Please, uncover to me what Brand car and size they drive?

_____

_____

_____

_____

_____

_____

13. Please, admit to me, are they married or single or divorced?

_____

_____

_____

_____

_____

14. Please, disclose to me their age group?

_____

_____

_____

_____

_____

15. Please, relate to me their gender?

_____

_____

_____

_____

_____

_____

_____

16. Please, impart to me which movies they attend and which theaters and what kind of books, do they read?

_____

_____

_____

_____

_____

_____

_____

17. Please, admit to me what they consume in soft drinks and alcoholic beverages.

_____

_____

_____

_____

_____

_____

18. Please, betray to me what they do for fun and in their free time?

_____

_____

_____

_____

_____

19. Please, indicate to me are they sexual?

_____

_____

_____

_____

_____

_____

_____

_____

20. Please, reveal to me which gym do they work out in?

_____

_____

_____

_____

_____

_____

21. Please, bring to light to me, are they generous with their monies and what do they love to spend on?

_____

_____

_____

_____

_____

_____

22. Please, impart to me a number amount, on how much they spend on every single itemized parts, of your Avatar?

_____

_____

_____

_____

_____

23. Please, acquisition 10 pictures of your Avatar from online and print it out and past them on the pictorial of your Avatar page.

Avatar

24. Please realize that, now we are truly ready to describe your Avatar again and compare the first description of your Avatar, to this questionnaires descriptions with as much detail as possible?

_____

_____

_____

_____

_____

_____

_____

_____

_____

_____

_____

_____

_____

_____

_____

_____

_____

_____

_____

_____

Chapter Eight

What is the formulation for being a prominent businessman and woman in the formats of being a conductor and not in the orchestra?

How is it conceivably possible to run and concert and direct, many greater companies and not let anything "fall through the cracks"?

Please realize that, as I was writing this sectionate segment of this chapter, a friend and a potential client, said this to me in his very frustrated view, of his vexatious business commercialism and in every factor, or antecedent of his business casualties and therefore, oy!!

You see, this man has been in business for so many impressively egregious years and there is no way that he is not prospering and successful. There is absolutely never a place, or time period, that I could have ever imagined someone like him, struggling and grappling with his businesses.

Please realize that, this is for me, hard to script...

This is his very sadder statement. "How is it even conceivably acknowledged and acquiesced and recognized, that we think that we deserve, or condign, being overwhelmed and we thereby, feel that we are subjugated and reliant under the cruelest regime and the worst possible compositions of nonsensical artistries and designs and configurations. We are subject to the unfavorable elements of everything, that I could ever have imagined in the business world.

Now in English.. how is it possible to work so hard and never stop chasing our tails?"

Ugh!!

By the way, this man is a friend and one of my potential clients.

You see, his exclamation and his verse confuses and radiates of such frustration and such star qualities of being involved in his company, in the exact ways, that I will guide you not to be involved, or direct, or just simply run your company. I will be forcefully admonish you all, to never ever be in that way, micro-managing and being in the orchestra, instead of being the conductor of any company, even a smaller one.

Please, realize that this is just the only venue and the only reciprocations and the interesting analogy, that I could have explained to you, what a billionaire and a very distinguished and articulate and an over achiever and surpassing most businessmen and his very also, well established and revered peers are feeling, everyday.

Imagine, that he is in this world as a greater businessman and he has about 40 years experience and still he is in this world as a survivor and a very terrible advocate of not relying on help, right away.

You see, this greater man is still talking...

"This is just the beginning and the very understanding, that with this guidance and up-grade and cure-all, that I will be receiving and acquisitioning, It is not physically importuned, or conceivably possible, that anyone could ever complete a full days revue by their selves in such greater companies, or in as many acquisitions, as I have acquired throughout these very arduous years and counting.

I conclude and conjecture and believe with certitude, that like the analogy of trimming your own hair, or lasering your own body, from the forward position, which is not conceivably probable, or possible..

You see, if I conceivably maintain and restructure and micro-manage and thereby, "be in the Orchestra" and operate and conduct, the majority of my businesses on my own and in my business performa, attribute so much of the company to being me, with many particles and mass formats and volumes of negotiations, or time lapses and the opportunities for accumulating and acquiring, so much more achievements, has passed me by.

You see, I am of opulent and prosperous means and a prominent personality and still, I have not truly enjoyed my wealth, or my luxurious milieu. I have been in a heavyhearted and vacated and abrogated community of wealth and destructive thinking, that with less help and with doing things ourselves, we will prosper.

I truly believed, in the PAST, that "if you want to get the job done, do it yourself".

Being in this environment, has debauched and has misrepresented our truer ways of conducting business and now, I am 65 years older, than I wished to be and I am a greater patriarch in my field.

Finally, after 38 years in my allocated vocation, I truly understand and I individually herald and of course, acknowledge that the only way, that I could have ever been successful, was to let go.

You see, I could of been in such a better way, in every single performa business acquisitions, that I had ventured into and I have would have not only matured and increased and propagate my sales, but I had the capacities, of being wealthier, if that at all was possible. Imagine that!!

Imagine, that I would have been in the formats, of being so much more astuter and adroit and smarter in every big league ways, of gainfully earning a living in this cosmos, of this universallies.

You see, I just learned that if you micro-manage your business and your professional practice, then you will just make your business, or your work place, smaller and modest and trivialized, in order to succeed.

Did you ever conceivably acknowledge, that there is just no way, if you continue to manage your businesses, in the exact ways that normal businesses are run, and maybe, thinking that you just need to adjust your businesses, to let it in the final portions of retiring and run by its self?

You see, I have a greater way of explaining to you all, in a prefabricated and straightforward way, of explaining that one needs to be a conductor and not in the masterfully planned -layer of an instrument in the orchestra...

One needs to be in supervisory responsibility and in charge and in the overviews in the referees parts, of doing business.

You see, as CFO's, we are in dire need and committal and a must to relinquish control to our employees, that we have credence and that we trust implicitly, in order for us to truly oversee the entireties of our overviews, from the conception until the final sales, of our very innovative and hopefully micro-niche product, or a service oriented business, as I just read.

I am a personification of a favorable junctures and opportunities and I have intellectually a paramount of information, to alleviate and be instrumentally and be an actively, easily present "conductor".

Trust me on this. I will never ever be just and inclusively, just in the orchestra, or the choir, ever again. Being in the orchestra truly incapacitated and relinquished my hold on everything, that I was truly executing.

So, lesson number one; Never again, will I micro-manage and not trust the main parts of my business, the managerial positions and the indescribably inattentive particles, of my being a wholesaler, to many major retailers and not in totalities understand and be informed, of every aspect of their price points, as well as for their culturally greater clientele, as well as many other aspects that I just read about...

You see, this is just the beginning for me. I feel rejuvenated and freed of my burdensome life and therefore...

.."you are hired', said by Donald Trump.

Thank you, for your greater support and of course, your intellectual input and confirmation, of what I truly and implicitly believe and affirm...

Please realize that, this performa is evident and has a plausible explanation and I am just expanding on what Deborah has said already..and it is through, an analogy of a conductor of a masterfully grandeur orchestra and an accompaniment of about 1,000 personifications, in an unabridged and complete in every aspect, of this portrait of an orchestra.

In the analogy of, when a person is playing a choice instrument in the orchestra, it is vitally necessary for him to concentrate and be engrossed and be prefabricating, only his particles of his greater song, or symphony, with his musical instrument as if he is the star or the leading player of that very orchestra.

You see, in order to play the accompaniment and his very most probably, ambitious and greater parts of his performance, with the accompaniments and equipage of his instrument, to perfection...

Imagine, that you are in the aura and in totalities focused and centered and fixated and definitely centralized, on your own greater harmonized Capella.

If this is the very greater case and there is never a moment, that you are not concentrating on your own venues, or your intrigue, or love parts of your businesses, or services...

.. get ready to drop the ball and Ker-Plunk! As in the game, everything falls through the cracks and you do not know where to begin, to pick up the pieces.

You see again, I will be explaining through this analogy, the correlation and metaphorically appropriate parts, in this very vitally and crucially important, to comprehend and thereby, get an understanding of the parallel understandings, of this metaphoric analogy that pertains to our businesses, in our truer formats of understanding.

When you own a company and you are "in the orchestra", by micro-managing the designs, or the productivities, of every department of your company....

You might say, "but I enjoy the fashionistá parts of my company." Or, "I am a designer and I should be the one designing. I do a better preliminary form and delineation, than my lead artist designer". Maybe, you think that you are the only one, that will get the job done and that your employees are not competent and not trustworthy.

Then fire them and try again. If your employees are not dependable and voracious, then they will just hinder and burden the growth and the expansions and maturations of your business. Plain and simple!!

You see, if I could have ever truly individualized and truly explained and elucidated to you, that being in this business world is if anything, but tense and immensely stressful.

We are needed to be advocates and promoters, of being leaders and being the "Conductors" of our businesses, instead of "playing in the orchestra", in order to truly be successful and flourishing. We are essentially and vitally required, to create an environment of progress and aggrandizements, of the naturalistically customary advancements and evolutions of our leaders and our business structures, to implicitly evolve and up-grade with the "times".

If we are busy writing, or busy designing, or restlessly bustling from department to department, giving more than our input and guidance and encouragement..

You see, if we are organizing and tidying, instead of hiring for that very parts of your business and every facet and constituencies of your business, there is no choice, but for your business to stay small and inoperable...

You just, can not handle, or command, or parlay more, place confidence and approbate and trust me on that..

Get ready, for the culmination and denouement and conclusion of this thought process..

If you are in the orchestra and the conductor, how many performers, or repertory employees, can you truly undertake to guide and conduct? At the most 5-10, if.

You just do not have the man hours, even in an allotment of 24 hour day!!

You will probably already realize, that this factor, is of the truer realities...

..If you have more employees, you might thereby, sense a semblance of your business truly being out of your control and command and containment...

...under duress and hardships.

With 5-10 employees, how exorbitant, or grand, can your business, or greater calling and purpose, truly be?

Be prodigiously greater, than you can conceivably imagine ever being and "duplicate yourselves" replicate and multiply your very noteworthy gifted expertise and endowments.

If you are in the fear zone...

In the apparatus, of being in the energetically lower stream energy conductivity formats, of fear, that unfortunately hinders our senses, from truly performing our very best..

You must please understand, that by the teaching's of your apprenticeships, of your greater techniques and methodologies, to your prominent parts of your systematically better personalities, employees of course, that are of the astuters and the overachievers and are the choice employees and are preferably sharper and of higher grade qualities, in your very valuable and for now, a better for reading this book, flourishing company, than anyone else, I recommend at this very point in this time period, to replicate and be able to teach your wares and your grandeur particles of yourself, and your very greater learned techniques, to these trusted employees.

Please, never be apprehensive of your employees embarking in a similar business.

You see, if you smile upon and accommodate and gratify your employees, with a greater respect and honor and considerations and the earnings and the pittance is part of the appreciation, as well as, by including them as partial owners in your organizations, or companies, rest assure, you have gained a loyal employee, that "has skin" or a better focus in your company and an appreciation, that he will be better engaged and he will be a superior achiever.

You see, he will actively achieve and procure and actualize, in a goal oriented fashionistá venues, and therefore, consummate and effectuate, what ever it takes to make your and now, also his business, as successful and fortuitous and prosperous and of course, as wealthy as possible and please, never forget that it takes about 10 years for this exact employee to be an overnight success, if he embarks on his own business venture using what he has learned from you.

You see, another aspect of respect and kindnesses and effective salary compensations, is that the most important particles of doing business, is to keep the energetically greater formations, in perfect cleanliness and flowing in the positively based formats, only.

Plain and simple, we need happy employees and a happy atmosphere.

Please be reminiscent and be ready to create and embellish a better work place and please never stop recreating and up-grading your, hopefully, micro-niche market and therefore, a for sure success parts of doing business.

You see, you thereby, will always be "ahead of the curb" and you will always be, the preferred vendors in your very niche field.

A standardization to pursue and to catenate and to assure loyalty in the work parts of your life, is by paying a more worthier salary and commission based particles, to encourage your employees to have heart and consideration and a diligence and a more valuable and a more prominent regard, for your company and thereby, get ready to have loyal employees, that finally care about your outcome of your company.

You see, I recommend, that they will also get commissions and only, in the NET programmations and therefore earn a profit, instead of being in the negative parts of owing monies, for inventories and other miscellaneous expenses, as we have talked about, after all the overhead, that was never accounted for.

So, this is what I wanted to tell you all...

In order to truly be in the major league and magnanimously prominently excelled and remarkably and prodigiously greater than you can ever imagine being, it is imperatively vitally important to "duplicate" yourselves, as we have talked about..

We are needed to generate and create and birth talent and expertise and adroitness in every sectionate department and sub-departments and in every paramount and primary and in the not so stand-out parts of your business, that are in reality, segment of a whole structure and just as decisive and important.

You must realize, that every aspect and idiosyncrasy of your business, has to amalgamate and unite and synthesize and react and contribute and therefore, meld together in perfect sync and develop and father a symphony and a Capella, that must be in perfect acoustic harmony and balance.

Good luck and please, really never forget, or dispraise, or lose sight of these very tried and true lessons, that I have toiled to create on my iPad.

Chapter Eight

Review

1. Please elucidate to me, what does it mean to be in the choir and not a conductor in a business formats? Please, give an esteemed example.

_____
_____
_____
_____
_____
_____
_____
_____
_____
_____
_____
_____
_____

2. Please, describe what is the trick and the fundamentality mass parts, to being a conductor?

_____
_____
_____
_____
_____
_____
_____
_____
_____
_____
_____

_____

_____

_____

_____

_____

_____

3. Please, imagine that you are about to be the,CFO a Fortune 500 company, with a minimum of 1,0000 personnel, how do you masterly be the greater quarterback Navigator, or Maestró Conductor and still have weekends and can go home at a normal hour and take vacation time and simply put..have a life!!??

_____

_____

_____

_____

_____

_____

_____

_____

_____

_____

_____

_____

_____

_____

_____

_____

_____

_____

_____

_____

_____

_____

_____

_____

_____

_____

_____

_____

4. Please, show us your fuller and complete schedule of your day, as you are that very CFO?

_____

_____

_____

_____

_____

_____

_____

_____

_____

_____

_____

_____

_____

_____

_____

_____

Final

Congratulations! You have made it this far. Please take your time and please really start your own Flagship Store, or a Business structure, or any formats of earning monies.

Final

Please realize that, you will still have to take the course on whichever venue you choose for a structural parts. There will be a wholesale module and a retail module and an E-Commerce module and a Practice module for the service oriented business and also, the developments of your business ideas, through the interpretation of a business reports, when We finish crafting these very books.. so, please be patient and get ready to start a true business.

Please, make sure to get a Real Estate Broker to show you spaces and store formats and make sure, to draw pictures to merchandise your inventory and even the layout in your store or businesses. Please, have a name and a web site and an email address and a logo and everything, that is required to open up a Flagship format of a business. Good luck

1. Please, create a Flagship store, or business, or online module, or any formats, with every parts that you learned from this book, or from your class. Please, truly do it for real. Make vision boards, for every parts of each and every part, that you know how do.

_____

_____

_____

_____

_____

_____

_____

_____

You see, this book is the first of numerous preeminent Business books and free enterprise formulations, to help our societies and our countries and our world at large, to manipulate and to assimilate what we have been doing already in the business aspects of the creations of multitudes of physical value and abundantly and notably greater wealth.

Please also, understand that this is just the opinion of my umpteenth star value, of being a better performer of the grandeur particles of being a businesswomen, in this transferably and in the unison with other greater overachievers in business and in life, as well.

You see, therefore, get ready for so much more value and so much more leisure time, instead of just always chasing our tails..

Thank you, for enjoying this work and book. We hope that you could achieve so much greater parts of being in any business, by understanding the fundamentalities and the infrastructure of so many particles of any Flagship structure.

Please realize that, between you and me, this is only the Genesis and so much more in addition has to be said and therefore, get ready to read my next few books, to help alleviate and to actualize a more confident and astute and knowledgeably greater and austere parts, of being such a greater addition to our societies culmination of giving back and recompensing to society and to create value and notoriety and individuality and creations and evaluations and productions and patents and new technology and in a robust and in a formats of being such a better pre-fabrication, of so many other evaluations.

Bless you and good luck

If you have any inquiries, please, email me at
BusinessTextbook@DeborahShaul.com

Printed in the United States
By Bookmasters